SURVIVAL GUIDE TO MOTHERHOOD

SURVIVAL GUIDE TO MOTHERHOOD

—

KAREN STUBBS

HARVEST HOUSE PUBLISHERS
EUGENE, OREGON

Cover design by Faceout Studio, Molly von Borstel
Interior design by Angie Renich, Wildwood Digital Publishing
Cover images © natrot, primiaou / Shutterstock

Previously published as *Survival Guide to Motherhood: Learn to Thrive, Not Just Survive*

Survival Guide to Motherhood
Copyright © 2024 by Karen Stubbs
Published by Harvest House Publishers
Eugene, Oregon 97408
www.harvesthousepublishers.com

ISBN 978-0-7369-9005-9 (pbk.)
ISBN 978-0-7369-9006-6 (eBook)

Library of Congress Control Number: 2023947086

Printed in the United States of America

24 25 26 27 28 29 30 31 32 / BP / 10 9 8 7 6 5 4 3 2 1

I dedicate this book to my four children:
Kelsey, Emily, Taylor, and Abby.

Thank you for allowing me to share all
our stories to encourage other moms.

What a privilege it is to be your mom.

Contents

Foreword

I REMEMBER EXACTLY WHERE I was sitting when I had one of the most all-consuming cries of my whole motherhood. I was on the side of my bed with the door closed. I was hiding from my toddler, newborn, and husband. The newborn happened to trigger this deep sobbing, but if I'm honest, it had been building for three years, and it all unleashed in a big way. I had tried everything in my power to help my baby girl nurse consistently, drink a bottle without barfing it all up, or to stop crying for just one minute. Larson had some serious colic and reflux, and I had hit my breaking point.

I realize now why the cries felt so deep in my soul. I truly have never loved something more than these girls in my entire life. And I've never wanted to do something more "right" with all my heart. I desperately wanted to fix this situation and was hoping either this screaming baby or baby Jesus Himself would physically write a three-step action plan for reflux on my bathroom mirror.

Sadly, neither of those things happened that day. But I do believe God entered a friend into my life right at that time. Her name is Ashley. All her babies had suffered from reflux, and she understood the maddening attempts to make those babies comfortable. Ashley didn't offer a miracle, but she offered sincere hope, godly encouragement, and some practical next steps. I didn't know how badly I needed those things to survive. Once I could stop sobbing and look up, I could see that God did provide an answer. And He has been doing that for the last 16 years of motherhood in so many ways.

About five years into my motherhood journey, Ashley introduced me to Karen Stubbs. I read her books and studies long before we became friends in ministry. She's that kind of mentor and author that you just simply trust. If Karen's name is on it, it's simply "add to cart." Her podcast is at the top of my list because it's the next best thing to sitting across a meal with her. It's probably a good thing we don't live in the same city because I would just show up at her doorstep weekly for a pep talk.

Just like Ashley did for me that day, Karen has showed up in my life to offer me sincere hope, godly encouragement, and practical ideas for this journey called motherhood. Many times she has reached across a table or FaceTime or phone call with the most caring eyes and told me, "Courtney, you can do this!" That's what we all need, moms! We need a real friend like Karen to remind us that we will survive. That we *can* do it! And we are not alone.

In this survival guide, you will feel like you're chatting with a favorite aunt or big sister. I love that it's not just one giant pep talk from Karen—it has pages filled with practical ways to survive motherhood. She has picked what really matters in the chapters ahead, from discipline to confidence and sanity. I love that Karen won't downplay the hard, or overspiritualize every moment, or toss useless tips your way. Instead, she pours her authentic heart for moms and Jesus into every page. We need each other, moms. Grab a copy of this book for a friend who is sitting on her bed crying over a newborn. Or to the mom in carpool who is crying over a teenager. We will survive this together!

Courtney DeFeo

Introduction

ALL OVER THE WORLD, moms are the same. Every mom loves her kids. And every mom wants to do this job well.

The crazy thing is, every mom worries that she is messing it up. Every mom wonders if it's always going to be *this* hard. Every mom feels lonely at some point. Every mom wishes someone would come alongside her to encourage her. To point her in the right direction. To remind her why this job matters.

I've been a mom for more than 30 years. I have four adult children, Kelsey, Emily, Taylor, and Abby. I now have six grandchildren (with more in the future, I hope). To be sure, I am blessed. I am letting you know how many children and grandchildren I have to let you know I have walked in your shoes. I have been where you are, and I understand. I know what it feels like when the weight of motherhood is squarely on your shoulders. I have parented through many days, weeks, and even months by myself while my husband was working.

I have felt the loneliness of motherhood.

My husband was a Navy pilot for 12 years and has worked for FedEx for 25 years, so I understand a traveling husband. I know that when your husband is out of town, everything breaks! I, like you, have experienced the joys of motherhood and the pain of motherhood. I remember full well that sinking feeling of, *I can't do this! It is too hard.*

But moms, you can do this job, and you can do it well.

I know because I've done it too. I am here to walk with you—to teach you what I've learned over the years. Why? Because I know this is a tough job, but it is also a rewarding job. And though we may never meet, I have a passion to help you in this season.

Years ago, God put on my heart to start a nonprofit ministry to equip and encourage moms—all types of moms in all different stages of life. Since I started Birds on a Wire, I have traveled all over the US and even to a few other countries to speak to and encourage other moms. Now our podcast and curriculum materials reach moms all over the world, from Australia to Canada, Europe to India. We have truly become a worldwide community of moms!

I have talked to thousands of moms, read and answered hundreds (if not thousands) of questions, and here is what I've learned along the way: All moms have the same foundational needs, just wrapped in different packaging. We all have the same insecurities, whether we're living in Atlanta, Georgia or Cape Town, South Africa. We all have the same desires, whether we're staying at home or working full time. We all have the same fears, whether we have one child or six kids. We all have the same hope to get it "right," whether we live in the city, the country, or the burbs. We, moms, all need the same thing: someone to walk with us as we do this motherhood thing the best we know how.

I wrote this book to be that someone. I want to pull up a chair for you over coffee, so that while we're talking about you and your children, I can reassure you that you are doing a good job and encourage you to keep going. I want to affirm that you are your child's biggest advocate, and you can do this! And I want to validate the fact that being a mom is hard work. When your child pushes back against the discipline you've chosen, it's not because you're doing something wrong; it's because you are doing something *right*.

I want to keep you company when your fears flare up. What will your child's future be like? No one knows except God. I won't patronize you with a pep talk that everything will be fine, but I will counsel you to walk with Him. Invite Him into your mothering days. Give Him a front-row seat to your mothering journey. God's perfect love is greater than all fear. When you're struggling with self-doubt, asking, *Am I enough for my child?* I will remind you that the answer is this: not really...but God is enough. God will be there for you and your child. He will guide you as a mom.

When you confide in me about feeling lonely, I will nod in agreement, because being a mom is often an isolating role. And not only when your child is a baby and you are glued to their every need 24/7, but also in their older years as your children are growing up and moving away. It can be lonely even when you are surrounded by people, including other moms! Of course, you feel isolated when you're stuck in your own mind, alone with the problems that your particular child is facing. You're afraid to invite anyone into the mess because some way, somehow, you feel like you have created this mess yourself. How could you possibly share it with others? I want to be a safe companion for you in that place—the place where you need it most.

When you whisper, "Whatever made me think I could do this?" I will smile gently. Every mom feels the pressure of trying to figure out her child's needs. Because you're not sure, you're always taking shots in the dark. The constant pressure breeds insecurity. Even if you're rocking it in every other area of your life, your toddler or teenager is bringing you to your knees on a daily basis. The thought is always haunting you: *Am I basically doing a good job, or am I screwing up my child?* You're not the only one questioning your competence and your sanity. It comes with the territory. I hope to teach you how to not just survive motherhood, but to thrive in it. And maybe even to enjoy it along the way!

Yes, in those long stretches of unending days that turn into speeding-by years, every mom needs a cheerleader. She needs the voice of someone whispering, "Keep up the good work; I believe in you. Don't ever stop fighting for your children. What you're doing matters more than you will ever know!"

Moms, I am in your corner. And this book is here to stand beside you. Think of me as your number one cheerleader, cheering you on from the sidelines, yelling, "*You got this!*" But I will not only be cheering you on; I will also direct you to God's truth. I'll encourage you to remember why motherhood matters.

So here's to every mom around the world in every unique set of circumstances—all of us together on the same sacred landscape given to us by God. I pray that over these next ten chapters, you will be equipped with a few new tools in your toolbelt, engaged with the thought-provoking yet practical questions at the end of each chapter, encouraged in knowing you're not alone, and empowered with the joy of the Lord.

Love in Him,

Karen

An ordinary, down-to-earth mom who got through
motherhood and lived to tell about it

CHAPTER ONE

Know How to Get Through the Day

I REMEMBER THE EARLY DAYS of new motherhood with my first child, Kelsey. I was so busy all day taking care of her, I hardly ever sat down! (Sounds familiar, right?) But when my husband, Greg, came home from work and asked me what I did all day, I couldn't name one thing I really accomplished other than watching the baby. How could that be? I was an intelligent woman, and she was only a baby after all. Why couldn't I get a few things done around the house while taking care of her? How hard could that be? But every single day was the same. If I got a shower in before 8:00 p.m., I felt like I was really winning in life. But moms, I did learn. And as Kelsey grew so did I. I think that is one big thing we all need to remind ourselves: we as moms will learn as we go; we will get better.

Being a first-time mom is hard. None of us really knows what we're doing; it's all new to us. Thank goodness for growth, right? Each month you will learn as a mom, and each month you will grow. You will get better, I promise. When you start to feel down about yourself, remind yourself of what's true: This is your first time being a mom, and you will get better every day. Sometimes just that little encouragement from yourself can make all the difference in the world.

I remember teaching a class for young moms where a mom sat in the front row, listening intently and taking notes on everything I was saying. It's as if she was trying to learn all she could as fast as she could. After class one day, she told me, "I graduated with a business degree from the University of Georgia. I graduated with honors. I helped launch a company and ran all the marketing and sales. So why are my children rocking my world? I can't seem to get through one day without meltdowns from them or me. Then I look at my husband's life and his world hasn't changed at all. It's not fair."

I encouraged this mom that she wasn't alone in feeling this way, but I also told her the truth—a truth I'd had to learn for myself too.

"It's not fair that your husband's world hasn't changed while everything about your world has. But you need to embrace where you are and stop fighting it. Once you embrace this new role, everything will change. Give yourself and your children a little grace because you are learning every day. But when you stop fighting what you're learning and where you are now, you'll find a new perspective, and with that, a new ability to handle it all."

This mom listened intently to what I was saying. She nodded, letting it sink in. "I need to adjust my outlook and accept this is a stage of life."

"Yes," I encouraged her, "and if you do that, you will be happier, and so will everyone else in your family."

I wish you could meet that same mom today. She is killing it in the mom world. She now has four children, runs a social media marketing company out of her home, and homeschools her children. She learned how to thrive as a mom and as a woman. But to do it, she had to change her perspective from the start.

One of the hardest parts of being a mom is the monotony of it all. It's not exciting, alluring, or even magical. Day in and day out, being a mom is the same old thing: wake up, feed the children, get them dressed, entertain them or take them to school, feed them again, put them down for naps, entertain them, feed them again, bath time, bedtime, hit repeat on it all the next day. As the children grow up, you swap out nap time with carpool time. This daily grind can be challenging and leave moms feeling like there must be something more.

Finding contentment can be a struggle for most moms. Life isn't what we dream of at times. Sometimes, it's just hard! What helped me the most in this feeling is when I realized that just because something is hard doesn't mean it can't be good. Yes, life can be hard and good at the same time. I don't know why I used to think that I should be happy all the time or that I should never struggle in life. I don't know if someone told me that or if I just made it up in my mind. Because the reality is, life is full of struggles and hardships, and motherhood is no different. Just because I have a bad day with my children doesn't mean I don't love them or I don't love being a mom; it just means we had a hard day. Keep in mind that every morning starts a new day—a new beginning. And with each sunrise you have new hope.

Children are like Crock-Pots. They take time to teach, to guide, to learn. That can be difficult for us as moms because we live in an instant world. We don't like to even wait ten minutes in a drive-thru line! But nothing is quick with a child. You cannot rush them. Some days it can feel like you're trapped in the movie *Groundhog Day*, with each slow and seemingly monotonous task on repeat. The good news is, that's normal. We need to slow down our mentality when it comes to our children.

> Children are like Crock-Pots. They take time to teach, to guide, to learn.

Think about it! Have you ever been running late? Maybe you're late to work, or church, or getting to the store. You tell your child to put on their shoes. Moms, doesn't it take them forever? They are moving at a snail's pace with those shoes! And the longer it takes them, the more frustrated we get, right? So we rush them. We push them. But when we do that, they start to cry. That's when we realize we're going to be really, really late. But moms, if we'll slow down our pace and give our children some time, it will help us and them in the long run.

I say that because I've learned it the hard way. I'm talking to you from 34 years of experience here. I know the more you try to rush a child, the slower they get. And I also know it's difficult to build in that extra time to give your kids. But it is worth it. Slowing down will help your entire day. In fact, it will help so many areas of your parenting.

In 2018, my daughter Kelsey was pregnant with her third baby and having major complications in her pregnancy. She had hyperemesis-gravidarum, which is severe vomiting and weight loss in pregnancy. At the time, Kelsey and her husband, Kevin, were living in California, where Kevin was a Navy C-2 pilot. Kevin was assigned duty in Japan for six months, and with Kelsey's sickness and two little children at home, everyone agreed it would be best if she moved to Georgia to live with us until after the baby was born.

Greg and I went from a quiet, empty-nester household where we went to the movies in the middle of the day (because we could!) and ate out whenever we wanted (because who wants to cook for just two people?) to a household of five, two of them toddlers. From being foot-loose and fancy-free right back to the trenches of toddlerhood!

When Kelsey had her new baby, Talon, she experienced several complications after her delivery, and she was in and out of the hospital for two months. When Greg and I had the responsibility of watching the grandchildren, this idea of "children as slow cookers" came to me. One day, when I was trying to get the baby to sleep, he was a little fussy, and it was taking him longer to drift off. Talon was a newborn, so I wasn't about to let him cry it out. That was for his mom to do when he got a little older. But on this day, it was taking forever to get him to sleep. I had a small window of time because the older two children were taking their afternoon naps, and if I could get Talon to sleep, I would have about two hours to myself. But there was no rushing this child to sleep. He fell asleep when he was ready, not when I was ready. And wouldn't you know it? Talon fell asleep exactly the time the oldest got up from her nap.

Moms, you have this same choice in every moment of your day with your children. You can fight against them and try to force them into your world and your way. Or you can realize that children are like Crock-Pots, and they take *time*. That day, I, as the caregiver, had to slow my pace down to a child's pace. And I had to do it over and over again. While those children were under my care, it wasn't fair to have them run at my pace. It wouldn't have worked for any of us. So I told my staff that until Kelsey was better, my first priority was the children, and I had to go at their pace. In other words, things had to slow down in every part of my life, or we were going to struggle.

You might be thinking to yourself, *This all sounds great, but how is it realistic? You can't just stop living your life!* I agree with that 100 percent. You can't completely halt your life to move at your children's pace. Instead, you need to find a pace that works for you and your family.

On more than one occasion, I've been guilty of growing frustrated at my child for not moving at the pace that works for me. Maybe I set out to do a project, but my child doesn't cooperate. They won't play by themselves or with their siblings, and it messes up my ability to get things done. So I end up getting irritated because I can't accomplish what I set out to do. But it's not my child's fault; it's my fault. Not because I set out to do a project that needed to be done, but because I expected my children to adjust to a pace that only works for me. That isn't setting any of us up for success!

So how do you set the right pace with the right perspective? By remembering, again, that children take time. In all ages and in all areas, you've got to give them the time they need to learn and grow.

Children take time to discipline. That's because discipline is a long-term concept. Children won't get it in one session. I mean, how many times have you thought to yourself, *Why do I keep having to have this conversation with my child?* It's because it takes time to train up a child! (Proverbs 22:6). I truly believe that's why in Proverbs 31:28 Solomon writes of a mother, "Her children rise up and call her blessed" (ESV). As children become adults, they realize how much time their mother put in. They see how she was patient with them. They recognize that she let them go at their own pace. And for that, they are grateful.

I know I didn't realize how wonderful my own mother was until I had children of my own. Then I saw so clearly how she put in time with me and my sisters, and it paid off. It helped me realize that I needed to do the same with my own children. Now, as a grandmother, I see the benefit of all that time, but I realize most of you reading this book have many years to go before you get to that point. My encouragement to you is simply this: Hang in there! You are doing a great job!

And can I just give you a quick word of warning here? As your kids become teenagers, they'll need time as well. Teenagers take time to mature and grow. You can't rush a teenager to act like an adult. They may *think* they're adults, but they certainly don't *act* like adults. You have to be patient with a teenager. You have to give them the time that they need. There is no rushing maturity. It moves at its own pace.

A mom of a teenage daughter once told me that her daughter kept getting into little fender benders with her car. The mom called me so exasperated, saying, "I know she's just not paying attention to what she's doing." Sure, her daughter was old enough to drive the car, but she wasn't yet mature enough to understand the consequences of making those mistakes while doing it. So I suggested a plan to help her daughter learn the lesson in a way that worked for her. I told that mom that the next accident her daughter got into, the daughter should be responsible to pay for the damages. The daughter had one more accident, and this time, her mom made her pay for the damages. That ended up being her last accident.

Teenagers have to learn on their own, and most of the time, life teaches them. I know this is challenging, particularly in the teenage years. We want to help them when we're ready, but we have to be patient. We have to let them come to us when they're ready. You can't rush a teen to open up, can you? If your teens are like mine, they usually choose to open the floodgates and talk at the worst possible times, like during a good movie, or late at night, or when you are in the middle of preparing a big meal for the holidays. Maybe teens do this to see if we are really listening or if we really care; or maybe they do it because they usually are only thinking about what seems like a good time to them. They're moving at their own pace. That's when giving them your time is crucial. But until they're ready for it, you have to wait. And while you're waiting, pray. Don't ever underestimate the power of prayer, especially during the teenage years.

The bottom line is, we as adults—we as moms—have to change

our perspectives on parenting. Changing our mindset will make all the difference in the world. We need to resist the struggle and embrace the time our children need. We need to slow our pace and get in step with them. We need to build in the extra time it takes to let them move at their pace. We need to do whatever it takes to make it work. Why? Because our entire family will benefit in the long run.

Here are a few practical ways you can find contentment as you navigate this new perspective on mothering.

1. Know the Work Is Worth It

There are many challenges in motherhood, but one of the hardest for me was continuing the work without seeing the reward right away. This slow pace of life that required me to be patient while my child was learning to obey, learning to have manners, learning to be respectful, learning to be responsible—it was difficult. It felt at times like my kids would never get it. I was worried that all my work was in vain. I want to encourage you that your work, your patience, your labor—none of it is in vain. Don't give up! Your child needs you to be long-suffering with them. I know it's hard. I know patience for their pace is difficult. At the end of most days, you are beyond exhausted.

When Greg and I were watching the grandchildren, we used to fall into bed at night so tired we could barely move. I felt that way when I was raising my four children too. But now that my children are grown adults, I can tell you without a doubt that all the work—the blood, the sweat, the tears—was well worth it. I see my children now, and I am so glad that I slowed my pace to put in the work when they were younger. Now I really see the fruits of my labor. I want to encourage all you moms out there struggling to put in the work now. You are running a marathon, and I am on the sidelines cheering you on! I'm yelling, "You can do it! Don't give up! You've got this! The work is all worth it!"

2. Joy Is a Choice

Living a life full of joy and fulfillment is up to you. We all know that a mom's life is challenging. But try to resist the urge to complain often about how hard it can be. Not because you shouldn't be honest (you should!), but because staying in that negative place will only make you a bitter person. The truth is, you can make just about any situation better simply by adjusting your attitude.

In 2002, Greg was recalled to active duty in the Navy after 9/11. His orders were for a year. At the time, I had four children, ranging in age from middle school to preschool, and the last thing I wanted to do was to parent those children alone. I started to go down a self-pity spiral. Greg told me, "You can do this. You are strong."

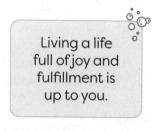

Living a life full of joy and fulfillment is up to you.

I told Greg, "I know I can do it, but I don't want to do it!"

The more I thought about it that way, the worse my attitude became. I started blaming Greg for being in the Navy in the first place. I thought constantly about how "selfish" he was. I will spare you all the details because they aren't pretty, but the point is, I was not in a good place.

One day, it hit me. My bad attitude wasn't helping anything. It definitely wasn't changing my situation; in fact, it was only making it worse. So I made the decision to adjust my attitude. I decided to choose joy.

I chose joy because my children were a little older during Greg's deployment so three out of the four of them went to school, giving me a little break.

I chose joy because I was working part-time at a church, and this small job gave me an outlet away from the home and much-needed conversations with adults.

I chose joy because I had great friends who encouraged me and listened to me.

I chose joy because Greg was not in harm's way while deployed, which gave me some security.

I chose joy because the children adjusted quickly. We had our days of course, but overall, they did great.

It was that simple. My situation was the same; I was still parenting four children by myself. What changed was my outlook.

I cannot stress enough the importance of your attitude. It makes all the difference in the world. And only you can change it. Do the heart work. In other words, examine your heart. Consider your attitude. If you realize it's not where it should be, make an adjustment. Don't get stuck on the fairness of it all. Get that thought out of your mind! It is not your friend, and it will not help you choose a positive attitude. Because the indisputable fact is, life isn't fair. In the mundane days of raising children, wake up each morning and embrace what's ahead of you with joy rather than resentment. You can't control much, but what you can control is your attitude. So choose joy!

3. Focus on the Now

Realize the importance of the slow days you are in the middle of living. Try to resist the urge to think that life is passing you by, because it is not. I promise, when you get ready to reengage in life at full speed, it will not take you long to jump back in. So focus on the season you're in now. Give yourself some grace. Celebrate the work you're doing and realize the importance of your job. Remember that God is the writer of your story. He is not limited by age, lack of work experience, or anything else you might believe counts you out in the future.

My career with Birds on a Wire did not start until my daughter Abby was a senior in high school. I worked part-time at a large church in Atlanta for 11 years and never once spoke on the main stage. After I left my job and started the ministry, a staff person from the church told me they never knew I could speak onstage. But God knew all along, and He is the one who gave me what I needed when I needed it.

Don't ever underestimate the power of God. Look at the people in the Bible we study all the time. They're all people God chose to use in a mighty way in God's timing, not their own timing. Look at Abraham and how old he was before he ever had his son Isaac. Look at Joseph and how he sat in prison for 12 years before God made him the second highest man in Egypt. Look at Noah and how he was an old man when God shared with him the plan to build the ark. My point? Trust in God's timing, not your own. Do the job you have been given today: raising your children. Treat being a mom like you are the top executive at a large firm in New York City. Give every day your fullest and do all you do for God's glory. I love the verses Colossians 3:23-24, "Whatever you do, work at it with all your heart, as working for the Lord, not for human masters, since you know that you will receive an inheritance from the Lord as a reward. It is the Lord Christ you are serving." Resist the urge to be anxious about tomorrow. Let tomorrow take care of itself; you just focus on today.

And can I let you in on a little secret? Social media is the enemy here. We can be doing great, and then we start looking on social media. We see how amazing everyone else's life seems to be, and we have trouble with the way our lives are now. Trust me, people might be posting amazing pictures, but a lot of the time, that is all they are: pictures. Reality and pictures are two different things. You know the old saying: "The grass is greener on the other side." Well, from my vantage point, grass is greener where it is being watered and fed. Water your own grass and don't worry about other people's yards.

4. Each Day Is a New Day

Moms can easily feel like one day flows into the next day, and there is nothing exciting about any of the days. You know you are in trouble when walking to the mailbox to see if you got mail is the highlight of your day. One mom confessed to me that she looks forward to the weekends, not because she has any great plans, but because her husband is home on Saturday and Sunday. It's another person in the house, and that is such a treat. Another mom told me that she takes long walks in the afternoon with the children just to escape her four walls and get a change of scenery. They're struggling to see each day for what it is: a new day.

Each day we have with our children is a gift.

Take each day as a new and fresh start. I cannot tell you how many times, when I was parenting my children, I went to sleep asking God to forgive me for losing my cool with my children that day, for not being patient, for being lazy, or for having a bad attitude. I tried to start every morning thanking God for the day and asking Him to guide my steps. My daily prayers usually started like this.

Father, thank You for this day You have given me. God, I ask that I would glorify You in all I do today. Each day is a gift from You, and I appreciate this day and all that it will bring.

Moms, when I pray that I may glorify God in all that I do, that means *all*. I can bring glory to God in how I rock my child to sleep. I can bring glory to God in the way I clean my house, speak to my children, or talk to my husband. I can bring glory to God in the way I talk to teachers, the way I drive, how I dress. I can bring glory to God in the way I guide my teenager, the work I do in my career, the way I prepare my child for college. I think you get the point. God is in our days—every part of them. Yes, even in the mundane.

Each day we have with our children is a gift. So when we have great days, let's celebrate them! And when we don't, let's remember that each day is a new day. A new opportunity to begin again. A new chance to glorify God in all we do as moms.

REFLECTION QUESTIONS

1. Growth can be hard to notice in the moment, but over the course of a season, it becomes clear. Reflecting upon your past few months (or even years), what's one way God has used this season of motherhood to change you for the better?

2. Think back to the times in the past week when you've felt stressed, frustrated, or inadequate. What sources of pressure are you putting on yourself—or your family—that lead you to feel this way? Which of those can you allow to fall away?

3. Just as you're watching your children face new challenges and develop new strengths, God is watching you do the same. What new challenges are you facing in this stage of motherhood? Can you see how God might be using them to strengthen you? (It's okay if you can't!) How can you ask Him to help you through these struggles?

CHAPTER TWO

Know How to Take Charge of Your Home

WHAT HAPPENED?

It's a question we moms find ourselves asking often, isn't it?

Some nights you go to bed feeling like you've got it all together. You seem to have a good grasp on the daily routine of your family. Everything is put away and in order. You're really killing this parenting thing.

Until you wake up one morning and realize you're not in control at all. Your toddler is calling all the shots, or worse, your teenager is changing the atmosphere in the family, dictating whether everyone in the home is having a good day or a bad day.

What happened?

Many moms go through their days feeling defeated because their house isn't cleaned, the mail is piling up, their child's science project is due tomorrow. And let's not even start about the laundry! Simply put, everything and everyone in your house feels a little (or a lot!) like chaos.

You know what can help you feel okay with that chaos? What can help you stay together even when it doesn't all get done on time (because honestly, it won't)? Taking charge of your own home.

Notice I didn't say "being in control." We are not in control, even when we think we are. But we can be in charge of our homes. In charge of the order or chaos, in charge of the atmosphere, the love that permeates through each room and the overall climate in our houses. A lot of moms don't think about this one point they just let things evolve. What if you were different? What if you were intentional about creating a home that reflected peace, love, hospitality? I think that is a home everyone would flock to, including your children. Instead of just allowing your home to evolve through the whims of a child, take this job of yours seriously and be in charge of the atmosphere in your home.

The truth is, neither your toddler nor your teenager needs or wants to be in charge of your household. But unfortunately, in many homes, they are. You know as well as I do that this disordered system doesn't work for anyone. And the only way to fix it? For you, as the parent, to take charge again.

Obviously, this shift doesn't happen overnight; it happens over time. You adjust your schedule, your routine, your happiness to accommodate the needs of your child. In other words, you give in. Of course I'm not saying there's anything wrong with giving in every now and then; it's just not good to do it *all* the time. That creates a pattern that will eventually cause you to you lose yourself and your home.

So right here and now, I'm giving you permission to stand firm and regain control of your home. You are the parent, and with that role comes the responsibility—the calling—to take charge. This is your title—your job. Don't let the chaos of everyday life steal it from you. Don't let your kids slide into the role of parent by accident or on purpose. Your home is just that: *your* home. So when you see it slipping out of control, it's your responsibility to take it back!

The best approach for taking back your home is to *parent smart*. And good news: parenting smart is something every mom can do! It simply means you're thinking a few steps ahead of your children at all times. That allows you to parent out of reason rather than emotion. It allows you to be a little more prepared to control the potential chaos that might threaten to take over your home in any stage of your kids' lives.

For example, when your child starts to crawl, you as the parent should be looking around the house to see what could potentially become a hazard for your baby on the move. Parenting smart means you cover up the electrical outlets, pick up breakables sitting on the coffee table or side tables, and remove any little objects that could be choking hazards.

Parenting smart during the elementary age might include being prepared when the children get home from school. More than likely they'll be hungry and filled with extra energy because they've been sitting in the classroom all day. So a way to parent smart is to have their snack ready when they walk through the door. Tell them to eat it then head outside for 45 minutes of play time. This solves the hunger and the energy problems before they start, allowing you to be proactive rather than reactive.

Now let's look at the teenage years. As your child enters high school, you want to create an environment that your child will want to invite their friends into. If you don't have anything like that already, be proactive and create some space for a teen hangout. Parent smart by setting up the space for your kids now. Then it's there when they're ready to use it. It doesn't have to be fancy. Just provide a space (and snacks!), and the teens will come. Here are a few ideas:

- In a basement, extra room, or in your garage carve out an area for your teenagers. Usually having a TV and some old furniture is great. You could also have a ping pong table, pool table, or maybe a high-top table with some stools.

- Give the den area of your house to the teenagers on certain nights.

- Create an outdoor space with a firepit, twinkle lights, and some music.

When my son was in high school, he had a close-knit group of friends. These kids were always looking for an excuse to get together. Whenever Taylor would ask if the gang could come over, my answer was yes. On Wednesday nights, when the show *Modern Family* was popular, it was a standing invitation for the gang to come watch at our house. Taylor would pop popcorn, and I provided some type of sweet snack and drinks. We planned ahead to make our home the environment we wanted it to be, and it worked!

Moms, I know it may feel like chaos in your home right now, but that doesn't mean it has to stay that way. You can take charge of your home, and you can start by parenting smart. When you think a few steps ahead of your child, you're giving yourself permission to be proactive and not reactive. And that, my fellow moms, will bring a much calmer atmosphere to your home and to your family!

Here are three steps you can take to help you start parenting smart.

1. Remember Who's Boss

Staying ahead of your children requires the right mindset—the one that remembers who's really in charge. You need to know that you're the boss so you can carry out your job with confidence. Children can sense when you're unsure, so be confident in your role. God has given you authority in their lives, so exercise it! Don't view this lightly. Step up and take charge. *You* are the boss of your home!

You might be thinking, *Karen, how can you say that so boldly? So unapologetically? I want to listen to my child. I want to allow them to feel the freedom to express everything they feel and be heard. I don't want to put restrictions on them or stifle their creativity in any way.* Believe me, I understand. But I can say this with boldness because God said it first. In His design, the mother and the father are the boss. God first tells us this in the Ten Commandments. You know about them, right? They are the big ones. Well, listed among them is "Honor your father and your mother" Exodus 20:12 (NASB). Then, we hear it again in the New Testament:

> Children, obey your parents in the Lord, for this is right. "Honor your father and mother"—which is the first commandment with a promise—"so that it may be well with you and that you may enjoy long life on the earth" (Ephesians 6:1-3).

We hear it a third time in Colossians 3:20:

> Children obey your parents in everything, for this pleases the Lord.

This isn't my idea; it's God's design. Of course you can listen to your child and allow them to express their creativity while still asking them to obey and respect you as their authority. It is *your* home. You have waited a lifetime to establish it, so be the boss.

Believe it or not, your children will feel more secure when they know someone they trust and admire is in control. Someone like *you*! See, whether your children are toddlers or teenagers, as long as they're living under your roof and you're paying the bills, you're the boss. You call the shots, whether they agree with you or not. More than that, while they're growing up, they need you to be the boss. They need a parent, not a friend. Friendship can come later when they're adults. While they're young, they need your wisdom, your guidance, and the security of a trusted authority figure to be the boss.

> You're the boss at home, but you'll only succeed if God is the boss of your life.

There will be times when your kids get angry with you because of your decisions as the boss. That's to be expected. When you take a stand, it will be hard. At times you will get pushback, so be ready. Sometimes it will seem like your kids are testing you every step of the way, but don't let that get you down. Remember God's encouragement:

> Let us not become weary in doing good, for at the proper time we will reap a harvest if we do not give up (Galatians 6:9).

It's true that being a mom is hard, but that doesn't mean you give up. Doesn't every job include things you don't like? The same is true with the job of being a mom. So rather than give up, rise to the challenge!

Remember: You're the boss at home, but you'll only succeed if God is the boss of your life. I would often tell my children that I was accountable to God—that I would have to answer to Him one day for my work as a mother. That gave me the courage and the strength I needed to handle any situation. Because none of us can do this mommy thing on our own. We need God to guide us as we guide our homes and our children.

2. Get Organized

If you want to know how to take back your home, the first thing you've got to do is get organized. Now, I'm not an organized person by nature, but when I force myself to think things through, it pays off in a big way. Bringing some organization to your life makes your job go much easier; it makes every part of your parenting feel more productive. And here is where parenting smart comes into play in a big way!

Think a few steps ahead. Look at your calendar. What are the variables of the week? Is your child teething? Your husband traveling? Do you have a big project to finish for work? Is it spring so you'll be at the ball fields three times that week? Is it a holiday season where you don't have enough hours in the day? All that stuff makes a difference.

If you find that it is a very hectic week, give yourself some grace and go easy on yourself. Listen, motherhood is a marathon, not a sprint, so pace yourself. You don't need to impress anyone; you are getting organized for yourself. Remember the object of the game is to take back your home and create an environment that brings you peace and rest as a mom. The more peaceful you are as a mom, the more that peace will trickle down to your children. So do yourself a favor and get organized. How? Well, here are some pro tips from my days as a parent trying to get ahead.

Get organized by planning a week's worth of meals. This will save you time and money because you'll only be buying what you need. Go grocery shopping once a week, or, if you can space it out, twice a month is even better! Just remember, not all weeks are the same. Start by sitting down with your calendar to see what's going on with your family that upcoming week. Plan with that in mind. For me, the weeks Greg was traveling, I would go easy on the meals. I knew I'd be burning the candle at both ends parenting by myself, so I went simple where I could. I'd make chicken nuggets, order pizza, cook breakfast for dinner—whatever was easy! Then, when Greg returned home, I would go back to more complex or robust meals.

Next, think about what works for you. I always let Greg help me plan the meals. I was always open to cooking whatever anyone wanted; I just didn't like to be the only one coming up with the menu. I also built in more of those "easy" meals for myself. I tried to always have a meat, a vegetable, and a starch of some kind. But no matter what, I always put one thing on the table I knew my children would eat. That helped avoid any eating stand-offs.

Once you've planned your meals, go to your pantry and refrigerator to write down what you need from the grocery store. Start your list at the beginning of the week and add to it as the week unfolds to make sure you get everything. Keeping a running list will help you remember what you need when you're standing at the store. This last step is what trips me up every single time! I *think* I have enough cream of chicken soup or chicken broth or potatoes but I don't. I know it takes extra time, but it is worth it.

Use your time wisely. Time is a game changer for moms. I mean, do we ever feel like we have enough time? That's why we must parent smart with your time too. When it comes to the time in your day, again, always be thinking two to three steps ahead.

Mornings can be the busiest time of all, whether you are a working mom or a stay-at-home mom. I think it's most helpful to be the first one up in the household. Wake up before your children get up, get your coffee, and take advantage of a quiet house to gather your thoughts. If you have enough time, get dressed while everyone is still sleeping. When your children wake up, I promise you'll be happy you had this time to yourself. You'll find yourself more engaged as a mom as the day unfolds.

In the afternoon, if you are a stay-at-home mom, get some chores done or work on projects while your children rest. It's such a great feeling when you accomplish something, even if it's as simple as cleaning out a cabinet! If you're a working mom, I wouldn't worry about getting projects done during the week. If you are working an eight-hour day, the last thing you want to do is take on more projects at the end of the day. Give yourself a break, and tackle those to-do items on the weekends.

If you are a stay-at-home mom, I want to give you some important words about using your time: You don't have to be your child's entertainment all day long. It's not your job to be the cruise director for your kids, planning activities, events, and play for every moment of every day. Actually, I think children should learn to entertain themselves.

As our kids got older, I encouraged them to play outside and use their imaginations. On summer mornings, if they came back in after ten minutes to watch TV, I would turn it off and say, "Everyone outside!" As they walked out, I would add, "You can't come back inside until lunch unless you have to go to the bathroom." Sometimes I even locked the back door. Our yard was fenced in, so I could always keep my eye on them while they played. After a while, I would often see that Kelsey had launched them into some wonderful make-believe story, and they were all acting out their parts. They would get so lost in their imaginations that when I finally called them in for lunch, they would answer, "Just a few more minutes!"

My point is this: I hear from moms all the time that say they don't have enough time in the day. The truth is, the time is there, if you are wise with it. Keep in mind that your work as a mom is never done! You will never finish all the laundry, the cooking, the cleaning, the picking up of all the toys—it is a never-ending job. Pace yourself. Be okay with not having a picture-perfect house at all times. Don't sacrifice your own time for the sake of a few chores. Because remember, the time is there, even for you to take a break!

When my kids were growing up, I had a rule that by 8:00 p.m., I did not do any more housework. I saved the nighttime to be *my* time. If I wanted to watch a show, read a book, or sit and talk with Greg, I did that from 8:00 to 11:00 p.m. Of course, I liked to go to bed with a clean kitchen, and most nights I did. But if I did leave a few dishes in the sink once in a while, I was okay with it because my me time was more important than a clean kitchen.

Give structure to your week. Create some predictable structure for your week. Put some plans in place that will be easy for you and your family to follow. While you don't have to live and die by the structure, it will give you some framework to think about and follow in big and small ways in your home.

For example, when my children were small, I would do certain chores on certain days. It was too hard to clean the whole house in one day, so I would spread it out. I know a mom with eight children who figured out a system that got her the help she needed in the week. She made a rule that when one of her children reached the age of eight, they had to become a contributor in the family. In other words, they had to start pulling their weight. Another mom I know who is a working mom saves all her chores for the weekend. It is too hard to work all day, come home, get dinner ready, and then do housework. So she structures her weekend to include those chores. And I have another friend who is all about the "chore chart." She gives out gold stars when the children help around the house, and at the end of the week, she rewards them with their allowance.

Bottom line: Whatever way you want to do it, make it work for you. Whether you're a working mom, a stay-at-home mom, or a mom with eight children, create a system. Find *your* system. It will make your weeks flow much better.

For me, following a daily schedule helped. Children love structure, and honestly I do too. If I know that afternoon naps are after lunch, I will make it happen. If I know bedtime is 7:30, and my children sleep better, I will make it happen. Having a schedule is so important, especially when your children are little. The best routine for your family might look different because every family is different. The important thing is to have a routine—one that meets your needs.

As you create your schedule, remember to include that me time we talked about. It's imperative that you carve out time for yourself. When our kids were little and Greg was traveling, sometimes I would hire a babysitter when I went to the grocery store. It was worth it for me to have that hour and a half to myself to enjoy doing a simple chore. Don't forget about you. In the long run, you'll be a better mom if you carve out regular time for yourself. You'll have more to give.

> Love and accept the season you are in, and find a way to bring peace in that place.

3. Create Your Home

Learn to create a peaceful atmosphere in your home that expresses your personality and taste. Remember, this is not just your home; it's your workplace as well. Your home is the place where you work, where you create, where you dream, where you rest. So make it into something that works for you. I am not talking about a designer home here. I am talking about a place you feel at peace.

I love the way a dear friend has done this in her home. Every time I visit her, I leave refreshed and full of ideas to include in my home. For example, when she decorates around the holidays, she uses leaves and greenery from her own yard. She usually has a fresh candle burning, letting that aroma fill her whole house. She writes simple Bible verses on her windows or a mirror in a bathroom. I asked her how she thought of that idea and she said, "I look out that window a lot when I am frustrated and having a verse there calms me down." It's what works for her.

I love music. It quiets my soul. So I always had music playing in our house as my kids were growing up. And eventually, my kids grew to love music as well. When they were teenagers, every bedroom would be playing different music at maximum volume. That's what they grew up with, so they learned to love it.

You might not like music or fresh candles, but you do like something! So learn what calms you down. Place that throughout your home. Make it a part of the atmosphere you want to create. Whatever your style, let it come out in your home.

Focus on *your* home and *your* kids. Don't be pressured to try to make everything perfect. If your house isn't picked up every day, life will go on, I promise. We live in a world where we feel immense pressure to live a picture-perfect life. But that is not reality. Life can be messy, so embrace the mess. Love and accept the season you are in, and find a way to bring peace in that place. I promise, when the children leave your home, there will be plenty of time to have cleaned-out closets, tidy spaces, and picture-perfect rooms. Create a home that's inviting and warm. The recipe will vary for every mom, so do what works for you. Take charge by creating the home that's best for you!

REFLECTION QUESTIONS

1. In what moments do you feel most confident as a mother? Why? What strengths do you have in these moments (e.g., knowledge, experience, compassion) that you can bring to or develop for moments when you feel less confident?

2. What are the most common ways you find yourself struggling with organization? Time management? Creating structure? This week, decide on one small change you can make or new habit you can practice that will help you improve in one of these areas. Tell your husband or a close friend about this goal, and ask them to check in with you about it at the end of the week.

3. What's something in your home that makes you feel *less* at peace? What change or fix can you make to this area so that it is no longer a source of stress?

CHAPTER THREE

Know How to Keep Your Sanity

THE DEFINITION OF *SACRIFICE* is:

> The act of giving up something that you want to keep
> especially in order to get or do something else or to help
> someone.[1]

A mom's world is full of sacrifice. Think about it! From the moment you found out you were pregnant, you began to sacrifice. When I was pregnant with Kelsey, my doctor told me not to drink Diet Coke! What?! Didn't he understand that was my one vice? The one thing I truly loved? Begrudgingly, I did it for the baby. In fact, I did so many things "for the baby" that by the time Kelsey was born, I was used to it. The idea of sacrifice for my child had just become second nature to me.

The sacrifices kept coming once she was born. Little did I know how much sleep would be sacrificed for the baby. I had no idea how my schedule would also be second to the needs of the baby. To be home for naps during the day so Kelsey would develop good sleeping habits? That was hard for me, and if I'm going to be honest, a little boring! But I did it, because I was a mom. And I knew that being the mom I wanted to be meant sacrifice.

As moms, I think we get so used to sacrifice. We get used to putting the needs of our children first all the time. It becomes second nature almost, so much that anytime we do put ourselves first, the big, ugly G-word comes into play. Yes, you guessed it: We feel *guilty*.

I wish I could see how many moms are nodding their heads in agreement with me right now. The struggle is real, ladies, and because it so real, I wanted to devote an entire chapter to it! Because it's that important to talk about how to not lose yourself in motherhood. Or better yet, how not to lose your sanity! If you don't pay attention to yourself, you can get so swept up by motherhood that you lose sight of yourself, and believe me, that is not good.

Just think for a second about all the ways a mom sacrifices. She sacrifices her body, her time, her schedule, her relationships, her money, her sleep. Even her work, her marriage, and her health can take a hit after children enter the scene! If we're not careful, moms, we can end up sacrificing it all.

So why do we do it? Because we want the end goal. The end goal of raising a well-balanced, healthy child who will grow into an adult who is loving, kind, responsible, respectful, and whose heart chases after God. Therefore, we sacrifice. We put our needs and wants on hold so we can give it all to our children.

When my children were young and money was tight, I wanted to make sure they all looked cute and were well-dressed. Of course, spending money on them meant I wouldn't be wearing anything new; it was all last year's styles. Let's be real, I was a stay-at-home mom, so I wasn't walking the runway either way. The point is, to give my kids what I wanted to give them, I had to give up something for myself.

And as moms, we do this all the time! You naturally sacrifice because you want the best for your child. When your baby is an infant, you start making sacrifices in your schedule. Why? Because we all know that a baby operates better when they're on a schedule. That means you may have to give up grabbing lunch with a friend or going out at night because your baby needs to be in bed by 7:00 p.m. As children grow older, their schedules change, and you gain a little bit of freedom back, but you're still, for the most part, tied to your children. Even if you work outside the home, you rush from work to go pick up your children from daycare, and you spend most of your evenings with them. You're sacrificing your free time because you treasure every moment you have with them.

I could go on and on. Because when it comes to sacrifice, moms never stop.

The rub comes when we look around and think no one else is sacrificing the way we are. Then we get angry. I'm speaking from experience here because I've been there. Usually the person I would get angry with was Greg. It didn't seem like he was sacrificing at all. But I had to realize, that is part of life. I hate to tell you this, but it doesn't change as your kids grow up. Remember that I told you how when Greg and I were grandparents, our daughter Kelsey had her third baby, Talon, and subsequently faced really difficult health issues? In that season, Greg and I were the primary caregivers of Talon and his two older siblings. We worked hard taking care of a newborn and two toddlers, taking on all the responsibilities that come with three children. But many times, Greg would leave for a week or so to work, and all the responsibility fell on me. When Greg was home, he worked as hard as I did with the children. He was a big help. He would take the children to school, fix lunches, change diapers, and more. But when his time came to go to work, it was all left with me. I had my work with Birds on a Wire too. I had to figure it out, juggle it all, and somehow make it work. That is the life of a mom.

Why am I sharing this? Because I want you to know that the feelings you feel are real; you're not making it up in your mind. But can you adjust your mindset to not be angry or bitter about the sacrifices you're making? Keep the end goal in mind in every season, realizing that the sacrifices you're making will pay off in the end.

> The healthier you are as a mom, the healthier your children will be.

I know I'm not telling you anything new. I know you already know motherhood is sacrifice. But there is a huge difference between sacrificing as a mom and sacrificing yourself in the process. It's imperative that while you are putting others first in your life, you not forget to care for yourself. As the mom, you need self-care so you can keep going. Because the healthier you are as a mom, the healthier your children will be. It is easy for moms to invest all our time and energy into our children and not even think about ourselves until we are well beyond empty. But when you're empty, you operate out of your weakness rather than your strengths.

I understand this is a fine line for us moms, and sometimes the line gets blurry. My advice is to do your best and to be aware. It is important that you periodically check in with yourself and assess how you are doing mentally, physically, emotionally, and spiritually. All those categories are imperative to your overall health and balance as a woman. No matter what season you're in as a mom, try not to let too much time lapse before checking back in with yourself. Do your best to make sure you are pouring into yourself on a regular basis.

And to help you do that, I want to focus on four specific areas you can focus on to maintain your sanity and help your well-being.

1. Mental Health

Your mental health is so important as a mom. And one of the ways you can maintain it is by keeping close people in your life to help you. Surround yourself with wise counsel. Proverbs 13:20 reminds us, "He who walks with the wise grows wise, but a companion of fools suffers harm" (RSV). I love this verse because it tells us that our friends make a difference. If we have wise friends, we will be wiser. Do you have a friend, a mentor, or someone in your life who will listen to you, speak God's truth to you, and guide you in His ways? If you don't have that person in your life, ask God to send them your way. We all get trapped in believing lies Satan tells us. That's when we need someone to speak truth to us. I have benefitted greatly in life from wise friends. A friend who is not afraid to tell me I am wallowing in self-pity. A friend who will tell me I am acting like a jerk, or being selfish, or being stubborn. A friend who will be loving and honest at the same time. This type of friend helps keep me from getting swept away in being self-absorbed or believing destructive lies. If you don't have that solid Christian friend right now, try looking into a certified Christian counselor. They can be very helpful in clearing the cobwebs from your mind.

For so many people, taking care of your mental health can come with a stigma attached to it. But listen, there should never be a stigma attached to something that makes you the best version of yourself. I think counseling is essential because it helps us process the hurts and tough situations we've faced in life. It equips us to navigate what we can't seem to push through. A counselor can come in, take an objective point of view, and help us get through depression, anxiety, fear, hurt, effects of abuse, and so much more. There is nothing negative about that!

See, the mental health of a mom is so important because you cannot give your own children wise counsel if you yourself are not in a good spot mentally. The healthier you are, the better advisor you will be for your child. What a gift a mom can be to her son or daughter when she has honest conversations with her child and admits, "I used to struggle in that area too, and this is what I learned." Wow! Think how life changing that could be for your child. Giving that gift of honesty and guidance to your child starts with pouring into your own mental health.

2. Physical Health

This area is probably my least favorite to implement, but it is so important in the life of a mom. Whether you belong to a gym, do workout videos in the privacy of your own home, or walk the neighborhood with a friend, the point is that you as a woman need to be moving in some way every day. I cannot count how many times I was down in the dumps and I put my child in the stroller to get outside and start walking the neighborhood. And honestly, that simple choice always helped me. We need to be moving our bodies, stretching, doing things to help preserve our physical health so we'll not only feel better each day but live a long, healthy lives for our families too.

I know exercise can be hard to fit into your daily routine, but try your hardest to do *something*. There will be seasons in your life when you can be more active and others when ten minutes is all you'll have to give. But no matter what, make it a point to care for yourself by moving. Your goal in caring for your physical health is simple: Always keep moving!

Now, let me confess. I am not a person that loves to exercise. I actually hate it! But the older I get, the more value I see in it. It also clears away the cobwebs and brightens our day.

Here are my top suggestions on how to get moving.

- Push the stroller around your neighborhood.
- Bike ride with your baby/toddler on the back.
- Pull a wagon with the kids in it around the block.
- Walk with a friend at night.
- Do workout videos at home while your child naps.
- Walk the track while your child is practicing sports.

3. Emotional Health

Can we be honest for a second? As moms, our emotions can be the easiest to ignore. We have so much running through our brains all the time, and that makes it easy to let our emotions run wild on us. The best remedy to keep your emotions in check is to remember this fact: Emotions don't always represent truth.

Once when Greg was on a six-month deployment, his ship pulled into port, and he sent me his hotel and room number. I called him one night, and he didn't answer the phone. I kept calling, over and over and over again. By the end of the night I had worked myself into a frenzy thinking something had happened to Greg. I was convinced that he was probably lying in a ditch somewhere, and no one knew he was hurt. In reality, Greg was fine. He had gone on a sight-seeing tour with some of his buddies, and when we finally talked on the phone, I saw how my emotions had gotten the best of me.

Can you relate? How many times have you worked up a situation in your mind concerning your husband, or a friend, or your in-laws? You may have convinced yourself they were against you or they didn't like you, only to later realize you were way off target. We have a tendency to project our feelings onto someone else when they don't actually think or feel that way at all. Emotional check-ins with yourself are huge in these moments. They'll help bring you back to reality and give you the chance to think about what's real. And in these times of emotional turmoil, you can always use a good friend who can speak truth to you and talk you off the ledge.

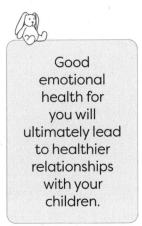

> Good emotional health for you will ultimately lead to healthier relationships with your children.

As a mom your emotional health is key to the relationships between you and your children. Think about it! If you've had a hard day at work and nothing has gone your way, and when you get home and your toddler spills their sticky juice on the floor, you are way more likely to react harshly. The quicker you can be self-aware of where you are emotionally, the better off you will be in interacting with and reacting to your children. Good emotional health for you will ultimately lead to healthier relationships with your children. And what mom doesn't want that?

4. Spiritual Health

I cannot stress working on this area in your life enough, especially in motherhood. My relationship with the Lord grew tremendously when I became a mom. Fear that I had never experienced before would try and grip me, but I held on to God's truth. In 2 Timothy 1:7, the Bible says this:

God has not given us a spirit of fear and timidity, but of power, love, and self-discipline (NLT).

Never in my life had I needed the things only God can give as much as I did when I became a mother! I needed the fruit of His Spirit—all the love, joy, patience, peace, faithfulness, kindness, goodness, gentleness, and self-control He could offer in abundance (Galatians 5:22-23). I don't think you can be the kind of mom you want to be without the fruit of the Spirit. I know my children liked me better when I was exhibiting those fruits. But you can't have the fruit of the Spirit unless you're walking and abiding with Christ (John 15).

Your walk with the Lord can be a game changer in your life. Moms tell me all the time that they don't have time to do a quiet time. I'm here to suggest that you can't afford *not* to do a quiet time. And who said it has to be quiet? Shout it out to God!

> *I need You! Give me patience with these children.*
> *Fill me with Your love, Your goodness, Your kindness.*
> *God, give me wisdom. I have no idea what I am doing.*

Whatever it looks like for you, it's imperative that you find time each day to connect with God and grow your relationship with Christ. Because ultimately, you need to be leaning on and gaining strength from the One who is in control.

Of course, I recognize that time is limited for you as a mom. That means connecting with God may have to look different depending on what season you're in as a parent. Along the way, I've found a few things that have helped me focus on my relationship with the Lord in creative ways.

- Place notes around the house with relevant Scripture.
- Go on a walk by yourself after the kids' bedtime so you can pray.
- Find just five quick minutes to read a short devotional.
- Play worship music in the house in the morning or in the car on the way to pick up the kids.

Whatever it looks like for you, don't take for granted the benefit of focusing on your spiritual health.

And overall, don't forget to pour into yourself as a mom. What happens when you don't pour into yourself? When you allow yourself to remain empty for days, weeks, months, or possibly even years? I believe you lose yourself as a woman. When the children start growing up, getting their own friends, or finding their own agendas in life, those moms who've lost themselves along the way struggle the most. They get so sad, full of despair because they feel their entire purpose in life is coming to an end. But listen, moms: Your life is more than just your children. Being a mom is just one part of your life. It's not nor should it be your whole life. It's never good for any one thing to be your whole life—not your children, not your husband, not your job, not your hobby. When that happens, it becomes your idol. Therein lies the danger.

There are many parts to you as a woman. You are a daughter, possibly a sister, a friend, a wife, an employee, a neighbor. Keeping balance in yourself sounds easy, but it's difficult. The mom portion of yourself can take over, so much that you forget to pour into yourself. You forget to pour into the other parts of your life that make you who you are. You end up continually putting yourself last. That, my friends, is a recipe for disaster.

So yes, while the sacrifices are real for a mom, they're not always going to be required of you in the same way. Eventually, this time of parenting will come to an end. Your children will grow up and move out to start their own lives. During the hard days of sacrifice, remember that this season of your life will end; you will again find freedom. But in the meantime, don't forget yourself. The goal is to not be empty when your next season arrives, but instead to find yourself full and excited to embrace it.

So allow yourself to practice in self-care. Focus on all aspects of your health. Pour into yourself. Do one thing for yourself every day, whether it is taking a walk, buying fresh flowers, taking a bubble bath, or reading a magazine for a few quiet moments. Sure, it's a small step, but if you will implement a little self-care each and every day, you'll find it will make a world of difference in your life.

REFLECTION QUESTIONS

1. Are there areas where you are feeling bitter and frustrated because you feel no one else is sacrificing the way you are? Take those areas to God in prayer and ask for His strength and a renewed outlook on the daily tasks of motherhood.

2. Do you have a daily or weekly routine where you can get up and move and take care of yourself physically? If not, what is the next step for you to start? What could you implement in your current stage of motherhood (nightly walks with a friend, pushing a stroller around the neighborhood, workout videos)?

3. What could it look like for you to find time each day to connect with God and grow in your relationship with Christ? If you don't have this time in place, which one thing would you like to try to begin to put into practice?

CHAPTER FOUR

Know How to Stay Connected with Your Spouse

I'M IN AN EXCITING time in my motherhood journey; my two youngest children are engaged and planning their weddings. What a happy, joyous time! I tell Greg all the time, "Love is in the air in the Stubbs household!" Isn't it such a wonderful thing? Seriously, a young couple in love? There is nothing better.

One thing I just chuckle over is how these couples in the engagement process seem to wear rose-colored glasses all the time. Everything is so "cute" and "adorable" in this season. Nothing is "annoying" and nobody gets on the other's nerves. I love listening to Abby, my youngest, and her fiancée, Ben, have conversations about their wedding. Keep in mind, Abby has been dreaming and thinking about her wedding since she watched her first Disney movie. Ben, more than likely, hasn't given it much thought over the duration of his life. Of course, Ben is excited and ready for the wedding, but he seems to feel pretty relaxed about the details. Needless to say, the wedding planning is a much bigger deal to Abby than it is to Ben. So when Abby is asking him a question about the details of the wedding and his response isn't as enthusiastic as Abby would like, her normal reaction is, "Babe, do you not care?" Ben, being a smart young man, always responds quickly with, "Oh yes, I care a great deal, but you do what you want."

Young love is great, right?

Now, if you're reading this book, then I'm assuming you are a mom of at least one child. So you know what it's like to be sleep deprived. You know what it's like to have conversations about the budget of the household and where you need to cut back to make ends meet. You know what it's like to juggle household chores with your career, your children's needs, and your spouse. You know what it's like to play the comparison game with your spouse. I remember once when Greg commented that he had changed three poopy diapers. My response? It was definitely less than loving. I told Greg, "Please don't act like you have done some great job in changing three diapers. You do *not* want to get into a comparison game with me over who changes the most diapers in this house. I will win." Sounds a lot different than those young love conversations, huh?

Here is the deal, moms: When you start doing life with your spouse, the rose-colored glasses come off and you hit reality straight on. That's when finding a way to connect with your partner suddenly feels more challenging than ever before. But trust me, it's imperative. So how do we do it? When we're caught up in taking care of the household, handling our careers, raising our children, how do we find time and energy to stay connected to our spouses?

After 38 years of marriage, I can tell you what I've learned. There are a few ingredients I think every couple can intentionally add to their marriage to stay connected in their relationship.

1. Dream Together

One thing I love about watching my children in this engagement season is the fact that they are hopeful and excited about their future together. They dream about what it will be like when they are married. They celebrate small things they're looking forward to in their marriage, like waking up with each other every morning. They dream about their honeymoons. They can't wait to set up their first households together. There is such a sense of anticipation and hope for their future with their spouses.

After being married for a few years, that excitement and hope for the future can leave us. It's not anyone's fault; it just fades as we begin doing daily life together. But the absence of it leaves a void. In marriage, we should always be looking to the future. We can still be excited about the possibility it will hold. For example, when we were first married, Greg and I would talk about trips we wanted to take before having kids. We would plan on when I was going to meet him on his Navy deployments. Planning for the future and talking about what we wanted to do brought us both so much joy.

In marriage, we should always be looking to the future. We can still be excited about the possibility it will hold.

When we started thinking about starting our family, we would dream yet again. We would go through all the conversations.

Would we have a boy or a girl?

What would it look like adding a baby to our family?

What changes would we have to make to make it happen?

Once again, dreaming for our future helped us stay on the same page. It helped us stay connected. It wasn't only my dream or Greg's dream to have a child; it was *our* dream.

As the years rolled by, Greg and I would talk about family vacations, our financial goals, anniversary trips to get away just the two of us. In all these conversations, my end goal was to stay as connected as I could to Greg so when the children went to college, we would be just as in love (or more in love) as we were the first year we were married. The last thing I wanted was to be in a relationship where there wasn't love or passion. I wanted a husband, not a roommate.

Respect Your Spouse

We've all witnessed those types of relationships, right? Relationships where love seems to have left. Now, it's just two people stuck in their ways, disconnected and not choosing to love one another well. Recently I was traveling home from a Birds on a Wire speaking engagement when I witnessed such a couple. I was sitting at my gate next to an elderly couple waiting for the flight. They looked like they were in their sixties or seventies and appeared to be returning home from a vacation. As I was sitting there, I overheard a conversation they were having about the return of their rental car. The husband was telling his wife that he had forgotten to turn in his papers for the rental car when they dropped it off that morning. The wife began to scold him. She said she couldn't believe he had done that and if they lost money because of his forgetfulness, she was going to be so mad at him. She then got up to go get something to drink.

While she was gone, her husband called the car rental place and explained to them what had happened. I could tell he was embarrassed. He sounded almost childlike while talking on the phone. The car rental company assured him that he had done nothing wrong. They would not be charged anything extra and all was good. The expression on this man's face when he hung up the phone was one of pure relief. When his wife returned, he immediately told her the good news. She replied, "Thank goodness you didn't cost us any extra money."

I know the woman sounds harsh in this situation. Your heart probably goes out to the husband. But that day, I remember thinking to myself: *How many times have I treated Greg the same way? How many times have I scolded him like he was one of my children?* It was painful to think about because I knew I'd done it before. When our children were little, Greg would ask them, "Are you ready for a bath?" They would always reply no. I would tell Greg, "Don't *ask* them if they are ready. *Tell* them it is time for a bath." Even in a situation as small as this, was I respectful toward him in my tone? No. And honestly, that didn't help our connection to each other.

This is my charge to you: Start noticing how you talk to your husband. Is it with respect and admiration? Or do you demean him with your words? If you are convicted about this situation, ask your husband for his forgiveness. Watch your words and your tone. He will not always parent exactly the way you do or handle situations the way you think they should be handled. Instead of correcting or resenting, be thankful that he is taking part in parenting with you. There are a lot of single moms who would love just a little help every now and then.

It is easy to focus on the negative, but it is very destructive to your marriage. And that will eventually spill over into your family life as well. Proverbs 19:13 talks about a nagging wife, saying she is like "constant dripping." I don't know about you, but I think constant dripping is annoying, to say the least. I don't want to be annoying to my husband. I would much rather be thought of as Proverbs 31:10-31 which says:

> A wife of noble character who can find? She is worth far more than rubies. Her husband has full confidence in her

and lacks nothing of value. She brings him good, not harm, all the days of her life. She selects wool and flax and works with eager hands. She is like the merchant ships, bringing her food from afar. She gets up while it is still night; she provides food for her family and portions for her female servants. She considers a field and buys it; out of her earnings she plants a vineyard. She sets about her work vigorously; her arms are strong for her tasks. She sees that her trading is profitable, and her lamp does not go out at night. In her hand she holds the distaff and grasps the spindle with her fingers. She opens her arms to the poor and extends her hands to the needy. When it snows, she has no fear for her household; for all of them are clothed in scarlet. She makes coverings for her bed; she is clothed in fine linen and purple. Her husband is respected at the city gate, where he takes his seat among the elders of the land. She makes linen garments and sells them, and supplies the merchants with sashes. She is clothed with strength and dignity; she can laugh at the days to come. She speaks with wisdom, and faithful instruction is on her tongue. She watches over the affairs of her household and does not eat the bread of idleness. Her children arise and call her blessed; her husband also, and he praises her: Many women do noble things, but you surpass them all. Charm is deceptive, and beauty is fleeting; but a woman who fears the LORD is to be praised. Honor her for all that her hands have done, and let her works bring her praise at the city gate.

I know this Proverbs 31 passage can be a little overwhelming for us women. We think to ourselves, *I can never be that woman!* Let me encourage you for a moment. You don't have to be that specific woman, but you can follow the theme of her life. Like her, you can be for your family, doing whatever it takes to make it work. You can honor your husband in all you do, wanting to please him and create a life that you both enjoy. The Proverbs 31 woman goes through life with intentionality; she doesn't just sit back and let the chips fall where they may. She plans, she works, she dreams, and she executes. We can all do that, especially with our husbands.

2. Work as a Team

I believe with all my heart we do not start out intending to belittle our husbands or to treat our husbands disrespectfully; it just happens over time. We get busy with life, and we take our frustrations out on the ones we feel closest to. I know it's your desire to have a strong, loving marriage—one that lasts over time. We all want to finish well. If we didn't, we would not have chosen to get married in the first place.

So what happens? Where does it go wrong? I believe many times it starts going south when children come into the picture. It's not that we don't love and adore our children—we do. But a struggle begins after children are born. The focus is no longer just on the two of you. And with that focus now split, tensions rise. Just like that, you tend to snap at each another more easily. You might feel that you are being taken advantage of, and he might feel that the children are now more important than he is.

The struggle for you is that often, moms are the primary caregivers for the kids. Dads are the heroes who walk through the door at the end of the day. Those two roles can leave you both feeling frustrated, but it doesn't have to be that way. You can bring your husband on board with you. You can work as a team. Working together is always better than doing it on your own. And working with your husband is certainly better than working against him!

Think about it from your husband's perspective. I believe it is hard for men to be away from home all day or sometimes for several days if they travel. It's difficult for them to know exactly when and how to jump in with the routine in your family when they return home. They want to help, but they just don't know how. This is where including them in the process will help.

> Working together is always better than doing it on your own.

When our kids were young and Greg was traveling a lot, it was hard for him to keep up with the ebb and flow of the household. Because of this, he would sometimes let things go with the kids that I wouldn't. To keep us on the same page, when he returned home, I would explain what I was trying to accomplish with each child. In the Navy, when fighter pilots come in from a mission, they debrief what they did on that mission. So for Greg and me, this was our debriefing time. In that time I would let Greg know I was working with Kelsey on obeying the first time and not arguing with me. I was trying to teach Emily not to cry every time she wanted something, but instead to speak up and tell me what she wanted. I was working with Taylor on not pitching a fit when I couldn't get to him quickly enough. He was learning to wait his turn. And debriefing it all with Greg helped us get on the same page.

If your husband is a little slow to catch on, be patient. Remember, he is not with your kids all the time like you are. When they act out, remind him that this is the behavior you were talking about. Once he sees it for himself, he will be able to detect it again in the future. You should be working together. You are not in competition; you are a team. It is so important that your children see you working together.

I have also been asked, "How can I be submissive to my husband and still be the one in charge when he is gone?" It is hard to wear both hats, but it can be done. I always looked at my job like I was the executive vice president of our home. Greg was the president. We would create the rules together, and then it was my job to enforce those rules when he was gone.

I always knew that he supported me 100 percent. If we ever disagreed on a situation, we would discuss it. But in the end, I would submit to him. (Honestly, I can think of only one or two instances when we did not agree!) I treated him with respect, and he trusted the way I enforced the rules while he was gone. He never lorded it over me that he was the one in charge.

Have Realistic Expectations

I believe many battles are lost because of our attitudes toward our husbands. We are with our kids all day, and when they come home at the end of the day, we look to our husbands to rescue us from the kids. If they don't respond the way we think they should, we scold them like we would our children. This attitude does not sit well with them, and they in turn stop trying to help. They feel like they can't do it right anyway, so why bother? I really don't believe it is a submission issue, but more of an expectation issue. We rise and fall on our expectations. We expect our husbands to come in and meet our needs. We expect them to say, "Thank you, sweetheart, you are the most wonderful wife a man could ever have. You have done such an amazing job sacrificing all day long with these kids." When we don't hear that, we get angry and lash out at them. Thus starts the crazy cycle!

You might be thinking to yourself, *What is the crazy cycle?* The crazy cycle starts with expectations. When your expectations are met, things go great. But when they're not met, you get angry. When you get angry, you we lash out. When you lash out, your spouse becomes angry in return. When they get angry, they shut down. And when they shut down, you find yourself with more expectations being unmet. It's a vicious cycle that goes on until someone stops and breaks it.

The only way to break it? By setting realistic expectations and communicating what those expectations are. Then you're both on the same page. And when your expectations aren't met, you've created space to talk about it in a calm, loving way.

Moms, I feel your pain. I understand exactly where you are, and I sympathize with you. But handling a situation the wrong way never makes it right. Most men just need to be asked to help; they need to know what's expected. Then they are more than happy to do it. Unfortunately, most women think that if they have to ask their husbands to do something, it doesn't mean as much when they do it. That's just not true. We have to let even that expectation go.

Celebrate Your Spouse

If you have damaged your husband with your comments or indicated to him that he is not that great at parenting, it's not too late to fix it. Instead of letting it sit, go to him and tell him you are sorry. Ask for his forgiveness. Think of the things he does really well as a father and as a husband and praise him for those. Celebration can go a long way in rebuilding a connection.

It's always a good idea to celebrate your spouse and make them feel special. Some things I have chosen to celebrate over the years in our marriage may seem small, but they made a big impact on our marriage. Greg was so creative with the kids. He thought of things that I would never think of. He played games with them in the car, and he made up these crazy bedtime stories that sometimes went on for days. He loved to make them smoothies when they came home from school. When he wasn't flying, he would get up early and make them elaborate breakfasts and lunches for school. He was usually gone for half the month, so when he was home, he made the most of his time with the kids. Those were things I celebrated about him. I would praise Greg for all those wonderful attributes and avoid pointing out the areas in which he was not so great.

Listen, most men love praise. Shoot, most women love praise. So if you want your husband to feel appreciated, celebrate him. If you want him to do something or to change an approach in the way he handles the kids, praise him even if he does it just a little. I guarantee he will start to respond to it and even work with you more because he loves the praise, especially from you.

Someone told me a saying years ago that goes like this:

> You can either love your husband or you can try to change him. Whichever one you choose, God will do the other.

I think that's true. I don't know about you, but I think loving is better than trying to change someone. I have never been able to change Greg Stubbs, not even for a day. Loving him is a much better option. Trust me, celebrating Greg over the years has paid off in spades.

Don't Be a Martyr

As I've said before, my philosophy is that I don't need to be a martyr. In *Merriam-Webster's* dictionary, the second definition of *martyr* is this:

> A person who sacrifices something of great value…for the sake of principle.[1]

I think a lot of times as wives, we sacrifice the value of ourselves because we start to believe a lie that tells us if our husband really cared, he'd see us drowning and offer help. Because he doesn't offer help, we simply can't ask for it. So we stay silent.

Ladies, I'm telling you from experience, your code of silence is not going to work. Men don't get it. They aren't watching the same movies we're watching, like rom coms or *Pride and Prejudice*. Men aren't mind readers. They can't understand what we want or need if we don't say it. So we have two options: We can continue to suffer in silence and let the years add up, or we can stop playing the martyr role. We can speak up and tell our husbands what we need and want.

If I need Greg to give me some praise, I say, "How do you think I am doing with the children?" If I want him to spend some time with me, I say, "I need a date!" If I want him to bring me flowers every now and then, I say, "It sure would be nice if sometimes when you come home from a trip you would bring me flowers to show you've missed me!" Instead of silently martyring myself, I express what I need or want. I ask for his help. I tell him what I'm feeling.

And you know what? It works! The other day I saw this written in the notes section on Greg's phone: *Bring flowers to Karen.* That might not sound romantic to you, but it sure was to me! It showed me that he does care. He knows it's important to me, so he wants to remember to do it. I really do say all these things because I know that as wonderful a husband as Greg is, he does not think that way on his own. If I waited for him to think of these things, I would be waiting forever! Life is too short for that, ladies. So don't be a martyr; tell him what you want.

3. Let's Talk about Sex, Baby

I cannot write a chapter on staying connected to your spouse and not talk about sex. Before you skip past these pages, hear me out. I have talked to hundreds of women about this very topic. You would be shocked (or maybe you wouldn't be) at how long couples go without having sex. I'm talking months. That is not healthy in a marriage. I am not going to say how many times a week you should be having sex, but I will tell you this: You need to be having it more than once a month.

Some of the excuses I've heard over the years for this lapse in sex life are legitimate, but even if they are legitimate, I think they have to be dealt with. In other words, you as the wife can do everything in your power to find a solution to the problems in your sex life.

If sex is painful, go to your gynecologist. Tell them what is going on and work toward a solution. There are a lot of reasons sex can be painful, and most of them have a cure. I know that can be embarrassing, but your doctor is a professional. They don't think anything about your questions. So just ask!

Maybe you're tired. That is 100 percent legitimate, moms, but you can help this one out. Of course it may take the help of your husband to take some of what's wearing you out away, but I would guess he would be willing to help if he knows the end goal! Talk with your husband. Decide how many times a week you'd like to have sex. Then agree that on the days you are going to have sex, he's going to give you some extra help. You may need help getting the children ready for bed those days. Maybe let your husband do the bath and bedtime routine while you do something for yourself that quiets your mind and soul. A walk at a park, a relaxing bubble bath, a jog in the neighborhood, an hour of time just for yourself—you would be amazed at how just pouring into yourself will bring you energy and rest.

Sometimes sex just isn't as good for you as the woman as it is for the man. Greg and I used to do premarital mentoring, and he would share that it usually takes a woman much longer than a man to get to her happy place. Greg would always tell the young men, "What are you going to do for her? It's on you to figure that out." A lot of the times, the man just doesn't know his wife isn't getting to her happy place, but once he knows, he can help. And if he can help her get her there, the sex life for both of them will improve because she will be enjoying it just as much as he does.

Be mindful that after a woman has a baby, it's normal for her sex drive to go down. I did a great episode on my podcast, *Wire Talk*, with Dr. Mike Sytsma about this topic.[2] In it, Dr. Mike goes through the reasoning behind why the sex drive becomes lowered for a woman post partum. Trust me, it's worth a listen! Just knowing that what you are experiencing is normal can bring so much hope to your situation.

Finally, pornography can get in the way of a good sex life in a marriage. Pornography is rampant among men, and the damage it is doing to our families is horrific. I have seen a married man sob because his addiction to porn destroyed his marriage and family. The shame this man felt was saddening. The struggle he experienced was real. Men and women can get help with this addiction and be restored. Once again, it is worth diving into to get answers and help.

I don't think marriage is all about sex, but sex is an important part of marriage. It might be awkward to talk about, but it is worth it in the end to do the work needed to have a loving, lasting marriage.

4. Choose Love

In marriage it is so easy not to believe the best in your spouse. It's easy to not give the benefit of the doubt and to jump to conclusions. But if you want to stay connected to your spouse, you must decide to choose love. For a marriage to thrive and not just survive, love has to be cultivated and nurtured. Just because you said, "I love you" years ago doesn't mean it's enough.

When I was in college and dating Greg, I was really into cross-stitching. After Greg and I got engaged, I cross-stitched one of my favorite passages of Scripture: 1 Corinthians 13:4-8. The verses in that passage were so beautiful to me, especially as I thought about my life with Greg and our future together. I hung that cross-stitch in our master bedroom for over 30 years. Every day I would read those verses and I realized how powerful they really were. I understood how hard they were to live by. Eventually these verses began to ring clear to me in a real way.

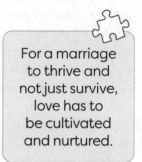

For a marriage to thrive and not just survive, love has to be cultivated and nurtured.

Love is patient. Patient when he is frustrating me. Patient when I want to scream and yell at him. I need to be patient with Greg when I feel he is not moving fast enough to suit my needs.

Love is kind. I need to choose to be kind to Greg always. Not just when things are going my way, but *all* the time.

Love does not envy. I can't be envious of Greg's life. I can't be jealous of the things he gets to experience that I don't.

Love does not boast or is not proud. I have boasted when the children might pick me over Greg. I mean, I wasn't overt about it, but in my heart, I was doing a little happy dance. But love doesn't act this way, and that's not how I want to respond to my husband.

Love does not dishonor others. When we love someone, we should build them up, not tear them down. How can Greg feel loved if I do not show him respect? Love means showing Greg respect.

Love is not self-seeking. This one hits a little too close to home. I don't need to be self-seeking, always demanding my wants and needs. We all have selfish ways, but in marriage, we have to choose to put the other first if we want to love as Scripture calls us to.

Love is not easily angered. I have to be patient with Greg. Love requires me to be slow to anger with him.

Love keeps no record of wrongs. If I am showing love to my husband, there should be no "I told you so" moments. There should be forgiveness.

Love does not delight in evil but rejoices with the truth. Love calls us not to delight in evil of any sort. It asks us to celebrate the truth of God. The truth that God first loved me, and because of His love for me, I know how to love my husband.

Love always protects. I want Greg to always protect me, and he does. Greg makes me feel safe, both physically and emotionally. My love for him protects in other ways.

Love always trusts. Love gives the benefit of the doubt. It believes the best in Greg.

Love always hopes. I need to have hope in my husband and in our future. I need to have hope that we will make it work.

Love always perseveres. I don't ever need to give up on my relationship with Greg. I need to always be pushing through arguments, differences, and conflicts to keep us close and strong.

Love never fails. Love doesn't fail through the hard times. It stands firm in sickness, financial difficulties, unexpected hurts, and small disappointments.

As we wrap up this chapter, I want to acknowledge that I know marriage is hard. But trust me, it's worth the fight. If your marriage is not in a good place, seek counseling. I have seen God do miracles in marriages when both parties were willing to do whatever it took to make things right.

You are worth the fight.
Your husband is worth the fight.
And your marriage will be better for it.

REFLECTION QUESTIONS

1. What's something in your life with your husband that you are still excited for? What dreams can you continue to share together?

2. What actions or strengths of your husband's do you most often appreciate? How often do you communicate this appreciation to him? In what areas can you encourage him?

3. What expectations, needs, or wants do you have for your marriage and family? Share those with your husband. What desires can you recognize and release as a result of unrealistic expectations?

CHAPTER FIVE

Know How to Discipline Your Child

NO MATTER WHERE I go to speak to moms around the country, I always get asked at least one question on the topic of discipline. And if there's time, it's usually more. Discipline is what trips up most parents.

I know it's tricky because it's tripped me up in the past too! But after many years of parenting, grandparenting, and talking to thousands of moms, I am here to share my best practices with you.

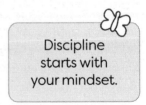

Discipline starts with your mindset.

Discipline starts with your mindset.

We have to keep in mind that obedience is taught. It does not come naturally, especially to children. I used to tell my children that we are all called to obedience. God wants children to obey their parents to obey God. As parents, our first priority is to obey God. I'll be held accountable to

Him one day on all things, including on whether I did a good job in teaching my children to obey. I guess this philosophy worked for my kids, because they never argued with me about it.

I love this verse in Hebrews:

> No discipline seems pleasant at the time, but painful. Later on, however, it produces a harvest of righteousness and peace for those who have been trained by it (Hebrews 12:11).

I thought this verse was so spot-on concerning my children. I looked up the word *righteousness* because it felt very formal to me. According to the *Merriam-Webster* dictionary it means *excellence.* That made a lot of sense to me! It is painful at times to discipline a child, but if I want a life of excellence and peace for my child, then I must do my job as a mom to get them there. And part of that includes discipline.

When you are parenting young ones, it's best to take your emotions out of the equation. Admittedly, this is very hard to do. But start believing you are the boss. Once you have established this in your mind, how do you get your children to understand it? You accomplish this not by yelling or threatening, but by *doing.*

In corporate America, we choose to obey our bosses because we don't want to be fired. We might not want to pay our taxes, but we do it because we don't want to go to jail. We obey, not because we want to obey, but because we don't want to pay the consequences that come with not obeying. You might be thinking, *Karen, I am not going to fire my child or send her to jail.* But hang in here with me for a minute. It's all about changing your way of thinking. If your child is out of control or not doing what you want him or her to do, it is almost always a matter of obedience. God has placed you in their life as the authority figure.

So, just like in corporate America, make the consequences for disobedience applicable so they choose to obey, even if only because they don't want to pay the consequences.

Now that you have your mindset, sit down with your husband and decide together what is going to be acceptable behavior in your home. This step is different for every family. For Greg and me, we didn't want to say no to everything. Instead, we focused on the three big Ds:

Disobedience

Defiance

Dishonesty

These were the things we decided we weren't going to let slide in the Stubbs household. Once you have decided what is acceptable behavior, gather the family together and have a meeting. (I called them Brady Bunch meetings in our house.) I would suggest letting the dad lead the discussion and explain the new game plan to the children. Make sure the children know that their dad is 100 percent in support of you while he is away. You are a team.

When enforcement day comes (and it will!), be consistent. Act before you lose your control. If you begin to lose your cool, put your child in his room until you can calm down. Then go to him and tell him why he is about to be punished. Tell him you love him, but disobeying is no longer an option. Tell him you don't want to punish him, but it's important that he learns to obey. You may have to enforce your punishments 20 times in one day at first. Realize your child is testing where the boundaries are. They're testing you to see if you truly mean business. Believe me, children are smart. You just have to hold the line one second longer than your child. The stronger the will of your child, the longer it will take, so don't get discouraged. Be consistent and show them you are serious about this part of parenting. Do not feel guilty. You are not doing anything wrong. In fact, you are doing it right. It takes time to train a child. Change will not come overnight, but it will come, I promise.

You might be thinking to yourself, *Why is disciplining our kids so difficult? Why do we have to tell them the same thing 100 times and they still don't get it?* It's hard because we are fighting with human nature. When your kids don't obey you, they are only doing what comes naturally to them as humans. They want their will to win out over yours. Sound familiar? This is not exclusive to kids. We know some adults like this, don't we? Maybe we're even that adult sometimes!

One benefit of growing older is that we gain wisdom. Life experiences can be a great teacher. As I think back over my life, I realize that whenever I insisted on my way, the outcome was never what I intended it to be. But when I obeyed God and submitted my will to His, the outcome was more pleasant. In the long run, it was exactly what I needed and even wanted. This principle of submission is a hard life lesson to learn, and our children have a hard time accepting it. Ask God to give you wisdom on how to teach this principle to our children.

Here is a real-life example of what the process looked like for me as a young mom. When Kelsey, my oldest, wanted something, anything— a new toy, a friend to come over to play, to go to the park to play, whatever it was—she would ask about a hundred times, and it would never stop. I would usually start off and explain to her why the answer was a no, and that maybe we could do what she was asking another day. No answer was ever good enough for Kelsey unless it was a yes. Well, one spring she wanted a copy of the Disney movie *Pocahontas*. I was actually going to surprise her with the movie at a later date, so I said no to her. In true Kelsey fashion she did not accept no for an answer and kept asking. After days of her following me around the house pleading, begging for the movie, I told her no, and that was my final answer. I told her that if she asked for the movie one more time she would never get the movie.

The next day, I was walking to the mailbox to get the mail and she was walking with me and said, "Mom, I've been thinking." I stopped her and turned toward Kelsey and said, "Kelsey please think long and hard before you finish your sentence. I want you to remember what we talked about yesterday." Kelsey looked at me, and you could see her wheels turning and she said, "Can I *please* get the *Pocahontas* movie?"

My heart was crushed. It was like she just couldn't help herself. But, I had to remain true to my word, and I said, "I'm sorry, but you will never get that movie now, because you brought it up again and I told you not to." The look on her face was pure devastation. But I have to say, that day she learned her lesson, and in the years to come, whenever I said no and to drop something she would drop it. It was a painful lesson but a good lesson to learn. I was very grateful especially when she became a teenager.

I cannot stress enough to you that discipline is important. I know it's tough, but if you think it's bad now, think about what life will be like if this behavior continues. Just add ten years to that temper tantrum your toddler is throwing. How hard will it be to deal with as a teenager?

Discipline for a teenager looks a little different. Obviously, taking away a movie isn't going to work at that age. But taking away the car keys will. Giving your teenager extra chores around the house—chores that are hard—works too. Our sweet Emily was not the neatest child. When she was in high school, we would constantly fuss at her about her room looking like a rat's nest. Emily and I came to an agreement that if her room wasn't clean by Friday morning before she went to school, her plans for the weekend would be canceled so she could spend all weekend at home cleaning her room. It only took one time for Emily to learn that I meant business. She left her room a mess, and I texted her at school to tell her to cancel her plans. There would be no going to the football game or on a date because she did not uphold her part of the bargain. She never did that again!

A lot of moms ask me, "How can you be consistent with your discipline when you are away from home?" The key to effectively disciplining while away from home is to discipline effectively when you are home. Your children need to learn that when you say no you mean no. If you are not consistent in your home, your children will play on your weaknesses in public. When my kids were young, I felt like I was being punished as much as they were. But for them to realize that I meant business, I had to follow through with the consequences, whenever and wherever. Be ready to take them out of a store or leave your cart to deal with your two-year-old's tantrum. When it comes to discipline at home or away from home, consistency is key.

> When it comes to discipline at home or away from home, consistency is key.

And moms, I know it's hard. Being consistent can be harder on you than it is on your kids. Remember, your consistency is going to pay off eventually. Say what you mean and mean what you say. If I tell my child that we're going to leave somewhere if he doesn't obey, when he disobeys, I need to pack up and leave. If I'm not willing to leave, I shouldn't threaten to leave. Because I guarantee kids will call a bluff every single time.

We also used what I call "creative discipline," meaning we found the right punishment for the right child. All children are different, so one way of discipline just does not work for all. I could give Emily a strong talking-to; she would change what she was doing and immediately apologize. Not so much with Kelsey. Kelsey was definitely my strong-willed child, so I had to continually show her that I was the boss. One punishment that usually worked with Kelsey was to make her go to her room by herself. Kelsey loved people, and she always wanted to be "in the mix," so being alone was torture for her. She had FOMO (fear of missing out) as a child. She would usually adjust her attitude and then join the group again. That punishment did not work for Taylor. He loved being in his room away from all the chaos. For him, we needed something else completely; we had to get creative. Taylor had a lot of energy and with that energy he would aggravate the girls probably because he was bored. What usually worked for him was running him around the house with extra chores. I would put him to work to keep him busy, and that usually did the trick with him. I'd encourage you do to the same as moms. Be creative with each child and do what works best for them.

So try different things until you find what works. I was talking with one mom who said that nothing she tried worked. In that conversation, I asked her what her child loved most. She thought for a minute and told me it was her baby doll. I said, "Take it away from her when she is not minding you." She responded, "I can't do that! Isn't that mean?" I replied, "If you want to get her attention, you need to take away something that she loves and will miss. Once you take away what she loves, she will change her behavior to get it back."

In two weeks, I saw the mom again, and she was thrilled to report it worked. "I couldn't believe it, but she started minding me," the mom said. "Now, when she doesn't mind, all I have to say is, 'Do you want me to take your baby away?'"

See, moms? You are teaching your children at an early age that there are consequences to their actions. So even if it's difficult, you can do it.

I know it can be easy to lose your cool when disciplining your kids, especially if they are not responding to what you're doing. But I firmly believe you should not discipline when you're angry. You could easily cross the line. Sometimes I would have to physically put my child in her room until I calmed down. I would tell them, "I'll be back in a few minutes to deal with you."

Once you remove yourself from the situation, it is easier to look at it objectively. Ask yourself these questions:

- Why am I angry?
- What do I want my child to do and why?
- What is the best way to accomplish what I want?

Prayer always helps too! God is a great resource in your parenting. Don't ever count Him out or think He is not interested. He created your children, so if anyone knows what makes them tick, God does. He knows what each child needs. He knows their futures, so ask Him daily what you should do to teach and mold them. Proverbs 22:6 says this:

> Train up a child in the way he should go; even when he is old he will not depart from it (ESV).

Each stage of discipline requires different elements from you as the mom.

I read this verse to mean that God has hardwired my child a certain way, and it is my job to work *with* what God has created, not *against* what He has created. God knows your children better than you ever will, so go to Him and seek His wisdom. Each day, lift them up to the Lord. Ask Him to give you wisdom in parenting them, and ask Him to bless them as they grow.

Now, are you ready to get really practical? Each stage of discipline requires different elements from you as the mom. Let's talk about the three natural stages.

1. Laying the Foundation: 1 to 5 Years Old

Foundation years require *energy*, and your focus should be on *obedience* from the child. During this stage, the mom and dad are establishing that they're the boss. Here, you are laying the foundation of your child's life. You can go back and correct the wrongs of this stage, but it is hard. So consistency is key from the start. Keep in mind, you only have to last one second longer than your child. I know it's hard, but if you do this stage well, it will pay off in spades.

To help, remember the three Bs:

Be Consistent

If you aren't consistent, you are confusing. People want to know why their child is an angel at preschool and a holy terror at home. The answer is because they know the teacher at preschool means what she says. The teacher has to keep order in the classroom, so she can't afford not to be consistent. Your child more than likely knows you will back down. Being consistent will solve that problem.

Be Clear

If you set a policy or rule in your house, don't change it. Shifting back and forth doesn't create clarity. If you say "No snacks before dinner" is your policy, don't change it. Even saying, "No snacks except for fruit, cheese, or yogurt" causes confusion. That isn't clear to a child.

Have your *say* match your *do*. If you say it, back it up. Not following through breaks down the work you've done to establish rules and consequences in your home.

Be United

Above all else, stay on the same page with your husband. Be united, especially in front of the children. If you aren't united, the children will learn to pit one of you against the other. Don't confuse the children on who is the boss; you parent together as a united front.

2. The Teaching Years: 6 to 12 Years Old

Teaching years require *time*, and your focus should be on *building your child's character*. During this stage of discipline, parents teach the why behind the discipline. This is a great time to introduce Bible verses that will back up what you are teaching your child. You're helping them understand why a behavior or choice might be bad or have a consequence. So the conversations should be, "This is *why* we don't lie steal, cheat, etc. This is *why* we want to treat others kindly. This is *why* we love other people."

There are no quick or easy answers; this stage takes time. When our youngest, Abby, was in fourth grade, I picked her up from school one day to find her upset. I asked her what was wrong, and she instantly started crying. She told me that she had lied to her teacher that day and felt so bad. I pulled the car over in the parking lot and listened to Abby as she told me what happened. I told Abby, "You need to go back into the school and tell Mrs. Martin that you lied and ask for her forgiveness. It is important that you face what you have done and make it right." Abby started crying even more. She said, "Punish me another way, but I can't tell Mrs. Martin!"

Here I had to explain the why. I said, "No, Abby, you need to ask for forgiveness. I love you so much that I cannot allow you to get away with lying because then, in the future, you will do it again. God tells us not to lie, and you need to make it right." I went on to tell her that if she didn't make it right, her heart would be a little hardened. That would make it easier to lie the next time.

Please hear me say that this conversation took a long time. I could have easily told Abby not to worry about it—that the important thing is that she was sorry. But I knew what was at stake. I made Abby go into the school by herself and talk to her teacher. She said she wouldn't do it, and then I told her if she didn't do it, she would not be having her birthday party the next weekend. Abby knew me well enough by fourth grade to know that this was not an empty threat. So she got out of the car, went to Mrs. Martin's class, and apologized. Mrs. Martin hugged Abby and told her she forgave her, explaining how proud she was that Abby owned what she did. Mrs. Martin assured Abby that she did not think less of her, but actually thought even more highly of her because she was honest. Abby slept well that night with a clean conscience and learned a very valuable lesson. It takes time, moms, but it is important.

3. The Coaching Years: 13 to 18 Years Old

Coaching years require *patience*, and your focus should be on allowing *actions to have consequences*. During these years, the mom and dad are still the parents, but they step back a little, allowing the consequences to play out in your child's life. In other words, don't rush to rescue them all the time. I know it is difficult. No parent wants to see their child fail. But remember, we all fail in life! It's important that your child realizes while they are still under your roof that no one gets a free ride.

As a parent, our goal is to get our child to the point that when they graduate from high school, they are responsible for their actions and can handle life. During these teenage years of a child's life, the parents need to start loosening control a little bit at a time. For example, in middle school, your child's schoolwork is their work, not yours. If they choose not to study or do the work, the natural consequences need to play out. You are not helping your child by rescuing them. Obviously you are still the parent, but every year as they get older, think of ways you can loosen your grip to give your child more freedom to stand on their own two feet.

When our children turned 16, they had to give us $1,000 for the right to drive one of our cars. This step gave our children ownership in the car. They had some skin in the game, which made them more responsible. Greg and I told the children it was their responsibility to take care of the car. We would pay for routine maintenance, but they had to take it to the mechanic to get it done.

Our family mechanic was amazing and agreed with this way of thinking. He would talk to the children and developed a relationship with them, so when the car needed work, our children would call him directly. We also emphasized the idea that if they were to get caught speeding, it would be on them, not us, to pay the fine. I think you get the point.

Once again, the goal in discipline is to have a responsible child ready to enter the world when they graduate from high school, whether they are going to college, trade school, or the work force. A child will never learn unless we allow them to grow and do things on their own. A child won't succeed without our help in disciplining and guiding them along the way. Read Hebrews 12:11. Discipline will never seem pleasant, but it will seem painful! God's Word tells us that it produces a great outcome for those who are trained by it.

REFLECTION QUESTIONS

1. Reflecting on your own childhood, how did you experience discipline? When did it impact you for the better? When did you perceive punishment as harsh, cruel, or counterproductive? Has your perspective changed now that you're an adult? How can you apply what you've learned from your parents' examples (both positive and negative) as you discipline your own children?

2. How does your husband partner with you in deciding when and how to discipline? Are you both on the same page about this topic?

3. Where do you see your child struggling the most to obey? How might you thoughtfully implement creative discipline to help them become better followers?

CHAPTER SIX

Know How to Be a Student of Your Child

ONE REASON PARENTING IS so hard is that every child is different. What works for one will not always work for another. That's why as a mom, learning your kids and making sure you are parenting each child the way he or she needs to be parented is valuable.

To do this, it's very important to know and understand your children's personalities. You cannot parent effectively if you don't understand your kids. Don't we all like to be heard and understood? Often when I am talking with Greg, I just want him to tell me that he understands my point of view. I don't think it's any different with our kids. I have four children, and they're all different. I can't parent Abby the same way I parent Kelsey, and vice versa. This is why parenting is so hard. If we could parent them the same way, life would be so much easier. But that just isn't the way it works. And that's why it's beneficial when we learn who our kids are if we want to parent them effectively.

You cannot parent effectively if you don't understand your kids.

Before we dive into the how of being a student of your child, let's look at the why. Why is it important to be a student of your child? Because, like we said, no two children are the same. Understanding each child and knowing what makes them tick is so important in parenting. Ask God for His wisdom (James 1:5). Ask Him for knowledge of your child, knowing that He is the Creator of each one. Psalm 139:13 says:

> You created my inmost being; you knit me together in my mother's womb.

Isn't it amazing that we have a heavenly Father who creates each of us in a special, unique way? Once we begin to see our children as God's unique creations, we can understand who they are as unique individuals.

I'm going to be honest with you: This will take a lot of effort on your part as a mom. But to have a child who knows their mom really gets them—a mom who understands the way they feel and think— is so powerful. I had to learn this the hard way with my son, Taylor. Taylor and I are complete opposites, so he really threw me for a loop. For example, Taylor did not like attention. He could be laughing at something, and when people would look over at him and comment on how cute he was, he would stop laughing and start crying. When we went to church, people would stop to say hello. He would either look away and growl at them or shout "No!" in their faces. Needless to say, I did not understand Taylor at all.

After several months of total confusion and wondering what I was going to do with this unsocial little boy, I pulled out the book *Personality*

Plus for Parents by Florence Littauer and read it for a second time. It helped me realize how Taylor was wired. I realized that he was not abnormal; he just did not like attention. It truly bothered him. So I began to work with him instead of against him. When we would walk down the church hallway, I would tell him that he did not have to talk to people, but he was not going to be rude either. I told him that if someone said hello or told him that he looked cute, he should just smile and thank them or nod his head. And guess what? Our new strategy worked! He didn't become a social butterfly, but neither of us was frustrated anymore. I learned to give him his space, and he became a happier little boy. Now as I look at him as a grown man, I am so glad I figured him out. We had a much richer relationship because of it! It wasn't always easy, for him or for me, but the time I put in as a mom paid off.

I write this to encourage you in motherhood. Some of our children we will just naturally understand. Other children will be a mystery to us. It's not that we love one over the other, but some may take more work. If we want a close relationship with each of our children, we can't give up on them. We have to commit to being a student of our kids.

To help you learn more about your kids, I want to look at the different temperament types we as people have. If any of this information catches your attention and you want to know more, please buy the books *Personality Plus for Parents* by Florence Littauer, *The Five Love Languages for Children* by Gary Smalley,

We have to commit to being a student of our kids.

and *A Grown-Up's Guide to Kids' Wiring* by Kathleen Edelman. I have also recorded several podcast episodes on *Wire Talk* discussing the temperaments to help you as moms discover how your kids are wired.[1]

My goal is to give you a high-level look at what the four temperaments and love languages are and how understanding them helped me as a mom. I do know they make a huge difference in knowing how to best understand your child. I've studied them for years and used them in my own parenting, so I can tell you from experience how much it helped me as a mom.

Below are the temperate types (and their associated color):

(Yellow) Sanguines

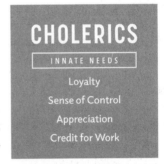

(Red) Cholerics

(Green) Phlegmatics

(Blue) Melancholics

The Four Temperaments

So let's dive into what the four temperaments are. These date back all the way to Hippocrates, and he used these words to describe them: Melancholy, Choleric, Phlegmatic, and Sanguine. I used these terms for years before shifting to use colors to indicate the same words.[2] So, from this point forward, I will speak about colors because they are easier to understand.

Yellow/ Sanguine
Key word: *Fun*
Get what they want through *charm*

For Yellows, life is a party. They love people, are very outgoing, and usually love to talk. They love to be the center of attention, and they love the spotlight. A Yellow temperament's key word is *fun*! It's easy to detect a Yellow because they use the word *fun* a lot. They say, "This is so fun! That's not fun! Let's do something fun! I can't wait to have fun." For a Yellow, fun is a way of life.

Yellows are very positive people, and they are usually a quick yes to anything spontaneous. To a Yellow, the sky is the limit. Even though a Yellow is a big dreamer, they won't always think of the details in accomplishing their dreams. Yellows will overcommit, say yes to everyone and everything, but they are such people charmers that they can work their way out from people getting mad at them. They get what they want in life by charming the pants off people with their fun, charismatic personalities.

I am a Yellow, and let me give you an example of how this temperament can work. When I was in second grade, I went to a Christian school in the Atlanta area. I went on a field trip to a Christian bookstore in Marietta, and I saw this beautiful plaque with a mountain range on it, made out of tree bark, and a scripture at the bottom. I fell in love and knew immediately that my mom "needed" that for her Mother's Day present. I went home, gathered up my money and went to the only driver other than my mom, which was my dad. I asked dad if he would take me to the store to get mom's present. Dad told me no because it was too far away. As I thought through how to get that plaque for my mom, I had the brilliant idea that my bus driver would love to stop and get it for me. In my mind, why wouldn't he?

So the next week on the bus, I sat behind my bus driver and asked him if he would stop so I could run in and get the plaque for my mom. My bus driver, like you would imagine, said he was so sorry but he could not stop an entire bus for me to grab my mom a gift. In true Yellow fashion, I did not give up, I sat behind my bus driver for the next few weeks, and reminded him I had my money, and I would run in real quick! After a few weeks of me pestering my bus driver, one afternoon, he pulled into the shopping center and said, "Karen, you have five minutes." Mission accomplished! The plaque still hangs on the wall in my mom's pantry.

Red/ Choleric
Key Word: *Control*
Get what they want through *anger*

Reds are your born leaders. They come out of the womb knowing what they want, and they do not mind letting you know. Reds are strong-willed and fight for what they want and for their opinions to be heard. I parented two Reds, and even though they were challenging, they have great ideas on how to get things done. The Red temperament is good with organization and leading people. Reds are very positive in nature and have a yes mentality to get the job done. They are hard workers and love to excel in what they do. This temperament is very task oriented and can be blunt and very direct in their communication. Reds are fiercely loyal.

They get what they want through their anger. Most people will give in to the Red temperament because they don't want to deal with their anger when they don't get what they want.

My sweet little granddaughter Harper is a Red. Since the day Harper was born, her Red temperament has shown through. When I'm playing make-believe with Harper, she is in full director mode. If I make a mistake in our tea party or imaginary scene she has dreamed up in in her mind, she will tell me, "Mimi, you aren't doing it right." Then Harper proceeds to tell me exactly what to say and what to do.

You never have to guess what a Red is thinking, because they will let you know. They do not run from confrontation; they actually like it.

Green/ Phlegmatic
Key Word: *Peace*
They get what they want through *procrastination*

Greens are easygoing. They roll with the punches and rarely cause trouble. They are your people pleasers. Greens usually are looking for the path of least resistance. Green temperaments love for everyone to get along, and a lot of the time they will be the mediators to find peace. Everyone likes the Greens because they are easy to be around. They have a hard time making decisions, mainly because, unlike the Reds, they are not opinionated. Because of their easygoing way, they can be easily overlooked. They make great friends because they are good listeners and they are compassionate. But don't let their good nature fool you! They also have a stubborn streak a mile wide. The key desire in a Green is peace. And finally, Greens control through procrastination.

Emily, my daughter, is my Green. For her tenth birthday, I suggested we go out to lunch just the two of us for her big day. Emily liked that idea, so we set out. We got to a crossroad and I stopped the car and asked her where she would like to go to lunch. She replied, "Where do you want to go to lunch?" I said, "It's not my birthday, it's yours, so you decide." Emily replied, "I want you to pick. I want you to like where we go." I said, "No, Emily you pick, it's your big day! Do you want pizza, burgers, Mexican, chicken fingers? You name it and we will go." Emily started crying, she said she didn't want to disappoint me and she just wanted to go where I wanted to go. We went and got Mexican.

Blue/ Melancholy
Key Word: *Perfection*
Get what they want through their *moods*

Blues are the thinkers in life. They are usually quiet and reserved. Blue temperaments like smaller crowds, and people can drain them. Blues like to be in the background in life, and they are not going to be seeking all the attention from others. They like their own space, and you need to give it to them. They are analytical and usually very methodical in their approach to life. Blues have a sensitive side to them and tend to be very thoughtful. A lot of them are creative or artistic. A true melancholy tends to view life from a more negative perspective. This temperament has high standards for themselves and others. Usually Blues are very good in school, and they will follow the rules. Blues are very self-reflective, and the Blue temperament's key desire is perfection. They always strive for perfection in life, but of course they never achieve perfection, which frustrates them. Finally, Blues control through their moods.

My husband Greg is a Blue. When we first got married, he came to me and said he had something he wanted to talk to me about, something was really bothering him. Greg was serious, so of course I thought I had done something major wrong. Greg told me, "It is really bothering me that you are putting the toilet paper on the wrong way." I started laughing, thinking he was making a joke, and then I realized he was very serious. So I asked, "What is the right way? I never knew there was a right or wrong way. It is toilet paper." Greg said, "The right way is over the top, and paper towels are the same way." I thought, *Wow! He is serious*. In a Blue's world, details matter, and they want things done right.

A few more tips concerning the temperaments:

Yellow and Green are relational people

Red and Blue are task oriented

Yellow and Red are positive people
Green and Blue are negative (or realistic, Greg says)

Yellow and Blue are opposite
Green and Red are opposite

Yellow and Red tend to be extraverts
Green and Blue tend to be introverts

So, now that you've got a basic understanding of each temperament, let me give you a quick example of how this plays out. Remember how I said Taylor and I are complete opposites? Taylor is a Blue and I am a Yellow. For me, life is carefree, spontaneous, and fun; for Taylor, there is nothing carefree about life—ever! One morning while I was driving him to school, I asked him what he wanted to be when he grew up. Honestly, I was just trying to make conversation. He answered, "It just depends on the choices I make over the next four to six years. If I make good choices and work hard, then I would like to be a pilot or an architect. But if I choose poorly, then I don't know what I want to be." Taylor was in the sixth grade at the time. Give me a break! I thought I was asking him a simple question, but in a Blue's world, nothing is simple. As a Yellow with a positive, sunny outlook on life, I couldn't believe his answer!

It's important to see the strengths and weaknesses in all temperaments. No temperament is better than another. And each one plays out differently in each child. If you have two Reds in the room, they will not always respond the same way to the same situation. That's because of any number of things, like their secondary color, their birth order, their love language, and their own uniqueness. We all have primary and secondary colors; I am Yellow/Red. Yellow is my strongest color, with Red being a close second. I lead out with fun, but I do have leadership in me. If you want to learn what color you are, or what color your child is, you can take a quick easy test on my website at BirdsOnAWireMoms .com/Quiz. It is important to know that every temperament has a basic desire. They each have needs, and they all get control in a situation by doing something different. Kathleen Edelman, author of *I Said This, You Heard That*, was the first person to teach me that every color had emotional needs, and I needed to study what the different needs were and give that to my children. Do you see what I mean by being a student of your child? I learned about the temperaments in 1991 with Kelsey, reread Florence Littauer book *Personality Plus for Parents* in 1996 with my son, Taylor, and then in 2011 I met Kathleen, who further educated me on the temperaments. Being a student of your child is a lifelong process. We never stop.

It is so important that you pay attention to the needs of your children concerning their colors. I have two Red children, and I cannot tell you what a difference giving them credit for their work makes in their lives. Again, for Taylor, my Blue, giving him space was key in his life as he grew up. When Taylor would arrive home from elementary school, he needed some time alone to recharge. The girls would sit at the bar in the kitchen and tell me about the highs and lows of their days, but not Taylor. Taylor didn't want to talk; he wanted to go down to the basement, turn on *Sponge Bob*, eat a snack, and completely veg out. Emily is my Green child who could easily get overwhelmed with life. She needed me to teach her how to deal with the stress of life and give her tactics on how to cope. I learned that if I told Emily, "Go clean up your room," it was too broad of a command for her. She would go to her room to clean it up and then just stand there doing nothing because she didn't know where to start. I had to give her specific assignments, like "Emily, pick up your dirty clothes on the floor, and when you finish come get your next assignment." Using these small tactics can make such a difference in your child's life!

Temperament Strengths and Weaknesses
Popular Sanguine
Yellow

Appealing personality	Compulsive talker
Talkative, storyteller	Exaggerates and elaborates
Good sense of humor	Dwells on trivia
Memory for color	Can't remember names
Physically holds on to listener	Scares others off
Emotional and demonstrative	Too happy for some
Enthusiastic and expressive	Has restless energy
Cheerful and bubbly	Egotistical
Curious	Blusters and complains
Good on stage	Naïve, gets taken in
Wide-eyed and innocent	Has loud voice and laugh
Lives in the present	Controlled by circumstances
Changeable disposition	Gets angry easily
Sincere at heart	Seems phony to some
Always a child	Never grows up
Volunteers for jobs	Would rather talk
Thinks up new activities	Forgets obligations
Looks great on the surface	Doesn't follow through
Creative and colorful	Confidence fades fast
Has energy and enthusiasm	Undisciplined
Starts in a flashy way	Priorities out of order
Inspires others to join	Decides by feelings
Charms others to work	Easily distracted
	Wastes time talking
Makes friends easily	Looks for credit
Loves people	Dominates conversations
Thrives on compliments	Interrupts and doesn't listen
Seems exciting	Answers for others
Envied by others	Fickle and forgetful
Doesn't hold grudges	Makes excuses
Apologizes quickly	Repeats stories
Likes spontaneous activities	

Temperament Strengths and Weaknesses
Powerful Choleric
Red

Born leader Dynamic and active Compulsive need for change Must correct wrongs Strong-willed and decisive Unemotional Not easily discouraged Independent and self-sufficient	Bossy Impatient Quick tempered Can't relax Too impetuous Doesn't shy from controversy Enjoys arguments Won't give up on losing Comes on too strong Inflexible Is not complementary Dislikes tears and emotions Is unsympathetic
Goal oriented Sees the whole picture Organizes well Seeks practical solutions Moves quickly to action Delegates work Insists on production Makes the goal Stimulates activity Thrives on opposition	Little tolerance for mistakes Doesn't analyze details Bored by trivia May make rash decisions May be rude and tactless Manipulates people Demanding of others End justifies the means Work may become his or her idol
Demands loyalty in the ranks Has little need for friends Will work for group activity Will lead and organize Excels in emergencies	Tends to use people Dominates others Decides for others Knows everything Can do everything better Is too independent Possessive of friends and mates Can't say, "I'm sorry" May be right, but unpopular

© 2018 by Kathleen Edelman

Temperament Strengths and Weaknesses
Peaceful Phlegmatic
Green

Low-key personality Easygoing and relaxed Calm, cool, and collected Patient, well-balanced Consistent life Quiet, but witty Sympathetic and kind Keeps emotions hidden Happily reconciled to life All-purpose person	Unenthusiastic Fearful and worried Indecisive Avoids responsibility Quiet will of iron Selfish Too shy and reticent Too compromising Self-righteous
Competent and steady Peaceful and agreeable Has administrative ability Mediates problems Avoids conflict Good under pressure Finds the easy way	Not goal oriented Lacks self-motivation Hard to get moving Resents being pushed Lazy and careless Discourages others Would rather watch No sense of urgency
Easy to get along with Pleasant and enjoyable Inoffensive Good listener Dry sense of humor Enjoys watching people Has many friends Has compassion and concern	Dampens enthusiasm Stays uninvolved Is not exciting Indifferent to plans Judges others Sarcastic and teasing Resists change

Temperament Strengths and Weaknesses
Perfect Melancholy
Blue

Deep and thoughtful Analytical Serious and purposeful Talented and creative Artistic or musical Philosophical and poetic Appreciative of beauty Sensitive to others Self-sacrificing Conscientious Idealistic	Remembers the negatives Moody and depressed Enjoys being hurt Has false humility Off in another world Low self-image Has selective hearing Self-centered Too introspective Guilt feelings Persecution complex Tends toward hypochondria
Schedule-oriented Perfectionist, high standards Detail-conscious Persistent and thorough Orderly and organized Neat and tidy, economical Sees the problems Finds creative solutions Needs to finish what he starts Likes charts, figures, lists	Not people-oriented Depressed over imperfections Chooses difficult work Hesitant to start projects Spends too much time planning Prefers analysis to work Self-depreciating Hard to please Standards often too high Deep need for approval Lives through others
Makes friends cautiously Content to stay in the background Avoids causing attention Faithful and devoted Will listen to complaints Can solve others' problems Deep concern for other people Moved to tears with compassion Seeks ideal mate	Insecure socially Withdrawn and remote Critical of others Holds back affection Dislikes those in opposition Suspicious of people Antagonistic and vengeful Unforgiving Full of contradictions Skeptical

The Five Love Languages

The five love languages are also important in parenting your child. Children need all five love languages communicated to them, but usually one will impact them more than the others. In the book *The Five Love Languages for Kids*, Dr. Gary Chapman says that a child will usually start to show his primary love language around age five. Up until then, children need all five all the time.

Physical Touch

These kids love to be hugged and kissed; they love to snuggle. As your child gets older, especially if they are boys, wrestling and just goofing off can be a form of physical touch. Abby's love language is physical touch, and she can't hug or kiss Greg and I enough. I used to tell her all the time that I wasn't going to allow her to date until she was 25 because she's so touchy. (I lost that battle because she got married when she was 24.) When disciplining these kids, a spanking is usually very offensive and can sometimes be too much. Two of my kids have physical touch as their primary love languages, and I rarely had to discipline them. If I gave them a strong talking-to, they would usually change their behavior and didn't oppose their love language.

Quality Time

This love language is self-explanatory. What this child wants is time, time, and more time with you! Not only do you need to be spending time with this child, but you need to be spending *quality* time. So sitting and watching TV will not necessarily be enough. One year for Kelsey's birthday she said that instead of a birthday party, she wanted to invite one friend to lunch with us and then go shopping all day at the mall. All day long, I went in and out of every teen store imaginable and watched as these two girls tried on make-up, jewelry, and clothes until I could barely stand it. When Kelsey and I got home, I was worn out. I went to my bedroom and turned on the TV just to chill out. The next thing I knew, Kelsey was in my room sitting on the floor next to me. After all that time together, I needed a break, but this quality-time girl still wanted to sit together a little longer.

Acts of Service

Acts of service is a love language about "doing" for other people. Abby also has this love language, and she is constantly cleaning her room, washing the dishes, sweeping the floor, and the like. She loves to be busy. She enjoys working for me, especially if she knows I've had a hard day. One time she brought some artwork home from school, and I hung it in the garage because it was too big to put on our bulletin board in the laundry room. When she came in from playing in the yard, she saw her artwork and was so happy that I displayed it for everyone to see. With that one little act of service from me, she instantly felt loved.

Gifts

The love language of gifts is also self-explanatory. Keep in mind that it is not so much the gift that is important, but the thought that goes behind it. One of my love languages is gifts. That means my feelings are easily hurt if someone forgets my birthday or if Greg has not put any thought into my gift. One Christmas I opened a present from Greg to find a pair of socks. Needless to say, I wasn't happy. The good news is, Greg is typically great at being thoughtful. When we were dating in college, he would come see me every weekend at Auburn. He would drive down to Auburn from Georgia Tech every Friday and then leave on Sunday. Every Monday morning there would be a postcard or a letter in my mailbox, telling me what a great weekend he had had with me. He would drop them in the mailbox before getting on the road to Auburn every time he visited. I do believe that is how he stole my heart. He was speaking my love language loudly. If your child has gifts as her love language, you can write a special note and put it in her lunch, or you can buy her favorite candy bar and give it to her as a treat at the movies. Remember, it is the thought behind the gift that matters.

Words of Affirmation

The last love language is words of affirmation. The child who has this love language wants praise. Affirming words will motivate him to move mountains. Keep in mind that your negative words to this child can be devastating. You might say something in passing that is negative, but this child will hold on to those words like they are God's truth. Watch your words!

Understanding each child and knowing what makes that child tick is so important in parenting. It's important to remember that they're wired exactly how God created them to be, and that alone makes them special. I tell my kids they are special and God created them for special purposes. As your kids grow up, they begin to realize they are different from other kids. They might tell you they wish they had blonde hair, or they didn't have freckles, or whatever. My Abby has worn glasses since she was 15 months old. Even after eye surgery, she still needed glasses. She came to me crying one day because a child in her preschool told her that princesses don't wear glasses. Abby wished she did not have her glasses. Of course, this statement from my little four-year-old broke my heart. After hugging and loving on Abby, I told her that God made her just the way she is for a reason and that He has a special plan for her. I told her that she was a princess and that her glasses made her even more special. In short, I reminded her of the way God made her.

And you can do the same for your kids! Remind them that God knit them together in their mother's womb and they are fearfully and wonderfully made them (Psalm 139:13-14), and that He doesn't make mistakes. Who they are exactly as they are is not by accident; it's by God's design.

REFLECTION QUESTIONS

1. When does your child surprise you the most? When do they confuse you the most? In what specific ways are they different from you? What do you admire or appreciate about them?

2. How do frameworks like temperaments, personality types, and love languages help you better understand your child and yourself? How can you apply this knowledge to the way you parent them?

3. Are there any love languages of your child's that you struggle to speak? How can you work on becoming more fluent?

CHAPTER SEVEN

Know How to Build Confidence in Your Child

I WAS CHECKING OUT AT my chiropractor one day and the receptionist asked me if my son was Taylor Stubbs. I said, "Yes he is. Why?" She then told me that Taylor visited the office when he was home from college and was such a fine young man, full of confidence and so well mannered. The receptionist told me that she hoped her own son would grow up to be like Taylor. I thanked her and let her know how proud we were of Taylor and how much I appreciated her kind words. As I walked away, I thought about how far Taylor had come from being the shy little boy hanging onto my leg and growling at people that he didn't know. It was a long road to bring Taylor to a place of confidence. As his mom, I would get discouraged. I would think to myself, *What am I doing wrong?* The fact of the matter is, I wasn't necessarily doing anything wrong. My son just happened to be shy.

As moms, we can struggle when our kids seem to lack confidence.

We see children who are full of confidence—who are not afraid of anything or anyone. We see how they carry themselves with boldness and ask confidently for the things they want. Then we compare that child to our child—the one who seems a little (or a lot!) less confident. Of course we think it's our fault. Maybe if we had done something different, our shy child wouldn't be shy. If only we'd done something to build their confidence, they'd be able to be bold, strong, and assured like those other kids we see.

Can I just remind you that shy doesn't mean insecure? Some children are shy—painfully shy—and some are not. An introverted, shy child doesn't necessarily equal a child without confidence. Some children are born with an extra dose of confidence, like my Kelsey and Abby, and others are not. As a parent, we have to be okay wherever they land on the scale! But I do think there are things we can do to increase our child's confidence. Just know that if you start out with a shy child, it might take longer to get there than it will with a child who is more of an extravert. I think every child can develop confidence, though. And what parent doesn't want their child to be sure of themselves?

The first concept we need to address when it comes to confidence is the difference between nurturing and enabling. I believe God created a woman—especially a mom—to be a nurturer. Moms are made to have compassion and encourage growth. But moms can be so good at this job of being nurturers that we sometimes get in the way of our children's growth. Though well meaning, we end up doing everything for our children. Then it becomes less of a confidence issue and more of an enabling issue.

It all starts when we give birth to our children. As soon as those little bundles of joy are placed in our arms, they are 100 percent dependent on us. Babies look to us to meet all their needs. We feed them, clothe them, keep them safe, and change their dirty diapers. We are their worlds; they cannot live without us. It's a wonderful feeling to have someone need us so completely. But some of us end up loving that feeling so much we don't want to give it up. We love and enjoy doing everything for our children. It creates in us a sense of purpose to our lives. Our natural sense of nurturing turns into enabling, and that enabling will eventually weaken the child and lower their confidence. Instead of the child learning to do things for himself, he will learn that you'll do it for him. That's not a recipe for confidence!

It is 100 percent okay to be a nurturing mom—a mom full of compassion and love. Who doesn't want to be that mom? And who doesn't want to have a mom like that? My challenge to all of you, is not to get caught up in believing that your child *can't* do it without you. Don't buy into the lie that they *need* you to do everything for them. Because the truth is, your child can do a lot! But for your child to grow and be confident, they have to learn how to do things by themselves. The goal is not perfection here; the goal is for your child to gain independence—and with independence, confidence.

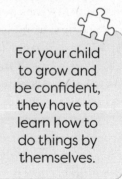

For your child to grow and be confident, they have to learn how to do things by themselves.

When I was having children, I was a Navy wife, and that meant that half the time I was parenting alone. I knew if my children weren't independent and didn't learn how to do things for themselves, our ship was going down quickly. First off, I was outnumbered four to one. I physically couldn't meet everyone's needs at the same time. So I developed little helpers, and most of the time my children were eager to do what I asked. I think the key in their positive attitude toward helping is that I trained them early. As soon as they could understand, I taught my children that being helpful and kind were the highest honors in the Stubbs household.

Kelsey and Emily were wonderful big sisters when Taylor was born. When Taylor was almost two, I noticed that he hardly ever said a word. I took him to the doctor to see if something was wrong with him, and the doctor said, "Karen, he has two older sisters who do everything for him before he asks. He has no reason to talk." The doctor was right! Kelsey and Emily would get things for Taylor before he ever let them know what he wanted. (Maybe I trained them to be a little too helpful!) After I realized what was happening, I told the girls, "I love it that you are so helpful, but Taylor needs to learn how to talk! So let's start encouraging him to tell us what he wants before we just do it."

That was just the beginning stage of learning to push Taylor. Trust me, it didn't stop with learning to talk. Every step of the way, I had to push my little shy, introverted boy. Taylor didn't like being stretched out of his comfort zone (which usually meant he was nestled right beside me). When I would drop him off at preschool, he would beg to go home with me. I assured him that he'd have a fun day and I'd be back to pick him up in a few hours. I would also do little things, like ask Taylor to go grab a box of crackers in the grocery store further down the aisle from me. Would it have been easier for me to grab the box? Yes. But would Taylor learn from that? No.

When he was elementary aged, I would let him order his own meal at our local restaurant. Even something as simple as handing his teacher a note from me had the potential to stress him out, but I knew deep down Taylor could do these things. Little by little, Taylor's confidence grew. He began to realize that he could do the uncomfortable things. And like that chiropractor, if you were to meet Taylor today as a grown man, you would never believe how shy he used to be.

Now listen, I get that I am a no-nonsense type of gal. I got that trait from my own mom. But I think any mom can instill confidence in a child and encourage them that they can do the hard things. It's not a matter of forcing them to do those things. You don't have to keep after them every day. Doing that will quickly shut your kids down and maybe even knock their confidence back a little, making them feel less-than. Instead, encourage them little by little. As in most things with parenting, you have to go at their pace, not your own. Then confidence can be built over time.

Maybe this is a struggle for you because you don't want your child to grow up in some ways. Don't we all want them to stay little in some fashion? Well, whether we like it or not, our kids are going to grow up. So rather than seeing confidence and independence as forcing them to grow up, consider teaching them confidence and independence a service. When my children graduated from high school and entered the real world, either by getting a job or going to college, I wanted them to be self-sufficient. In other words, I wanted them to do their own laundry, cook meals for themselves, be able to register for classes on their own, know how to manage their time, and be responsible with their schoolwork. And if I had done everything for them the whole time they were growing up, they'd be lost when they hit life on their own. As a parent, it's a great feeling to know that when you send them out into the world, they can do it.

Many parents stop short. The child brings home an assignment from school, and the child is naturally overwhelmed. It is a lot of work! But when that happens, it's better for you, the parent, to guide your child. Show them how to break the project down and take it in smaller increments. Whatever you do, don't just do it for them. With every step of the project the child completes, the child's confidence grows. When Emily was in the third grade, she did a school project on the state of Georgia. She did all the research and drew the maps and pictures all by herself. It was awesome. There were some children whose projects looked better than Emily's, but their parents had helped them. Emily did her project 100 percent on her own. She made an A and was so proud of her work.

It's a long process, moms! Remember, your child is a Crock-Pot, not an Instant Pot. Along the way, your child will mess up. They will cry and complain and tell you, "I can't do it!" Be patient with them and keep pushing forward. When your child messes up (and they will!), don't bail them out.

When Taylor was in fourth grade, he came to me and told me he had failed a test. Taylor was a smart boy and usually made great grades. Him failing a test was not normal for him. When I asked Taylor what happened, he told me that he didn't study; he thought he knew what he needed to know. He said, "I guess I didn't know it." So, I asked Taylor, "What did you learn?" Taylor responded, "I need to study." Lesson learned. Taylor didn't need a lecture from me. He didn't need me to punish him; he had punished himself. He learned from his mistake, and that is what growing up is all about.

I wanted my children to mess up while they were under my roof. I wanted them to get caught when they were doing something they shouldn't be doing. While they were under my care, I knew I'd be able to pull alongside them and guide them to correct their ways. Having perfect children was never the goal. Perfect children don't exist. But confident children do exist. And that's what I wanted my kids to be.

Kids' self-confidence is built when they take responsibility for their own projects, but you are also teaching them how to make decisions and think for themselves. Once again, I wanted my kids to be prepared for college when they were 18. I wanted them to be able to make their own decisions and not to be dependent on others. This process of developing independence is built over time, so the more I can give them to handle, the better off they will be.

Usually, good choices bring good consequences and bad choices bring bad consequences. Allow your kids to make choices because that is one of the ways they learn. I can tell them a thousand times to put their shoes away when they take them off. But if I hide their shoes and make them pay me a dollar to get them back, they learn much quicker. (I've done that, and it works! I've also charged a dollar for unmade beds, wet towels on the floor, etc. It's amazing how money motivates!) Money is another way to teach responsibility, which in turn builds confidence. The more ownership you give your kids, the more responsible they will become.

When our children were young, we planned a trip to Disney World. We began to plan our trip one year in advance. Greg made a chart for how much money we needed to save every month. He even put big Mickey Mouse ears at the top of our thermometer! We decided to involve the kids in the process of planning and saving for the trip. It was going to cost a lot of money, and we wanted them to learn how to save for a goal. We told them that we would cover the two hotel rooms and all the meals. They would have to buy any souvenirs or snacks with their own money. We were all busy saving, and it was fun to watch the red in the thermometer go up each month.

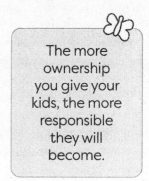

The more ownership you give your kids, the more responsible they will become.

On that trip, we had the best vacation we've ever had. While we were in the parks, the kids would say, "Can I have an ice cream?" I would say, "Sure, if you have the money and want an ice cream, go ahead and get one." It was wonderful! They were not constantly asking for snacks and drinks because they were paying for them. They were suddenly very aware of how expensive things were. And the best part of our vacation was that when we got home, everything was paid for!

Along the way, I learned that if my kids put their own money into something, they treated it better. They had some ownership and confidence because of the responsibility they had. I also learned a trick from a dear friend who had older children. She paid for their school activities and church camps, but she made them pay for any extracurricular activities with their friends. It was amazing to see how selective they'd be when they were the ones paying.

Be creative in your approach to building independence and self-confidence. Take into account what works best. What works for one child will not always work for another. There is no rulebook to follow. I wish there were, but that is why you need your heavenly Father to help guide you and give you wisdom. Don't try to do it alone! Lean on God to build your confidence and trust Him to guide you as you build the confidence of your children.

Okay, enough talk! Let's put it to work! Here are some guidelines for teaching your children independence and confidence at every age.

Tasks for the Toddler Years

2 years old

- Make their beds. (When I say "make their beds," keep in mind, I'm talking about just pulling the sheet and cover up to the top of the bed.)
- Pick out clothes to wear.

3 years old

- Unload and put away the Tupperware from the dishwasher.
- Help fold the hand towels and washcloths.
- Help pick up sticks in the yard before someone else cuts the grass.

4 years old

- Unload and put away all the silverware in the dishwasher.

- Clean the windows by the front door.

- Feed the pets.

5 years old

- Help set the table for dinner.

- Help clear the table.

- Help with the dusting.

Tasks for the Elementary Years

- Set and clear the table.

- Bring dirty clothes to the laundry room.

- Clean the toilets and sinks.

- Sweep out the garage.

- By third grade, children should be responsible for their homework.

Tasks for the Middle School Years

- Cut the grass.

- Wash the car.

- Vacuum.

- Do laundry.

- Care for the pets.

Tasks for the High School Years

- Pay for gas for their cars.
- Take care of the cars they drive.
- Complete all homework and keep Mom and Dad informed about grades.
- Apply to colleges when the time is right.
- Manage their schedules.

REFLECTION QUESTIONS

1. In what areas is your child confident already? In what areas are they still growing? Are there any specific steps you can take to encourage them in these areas?

2. When do you have the hardest time allowing your child to work or struggle through a situation on their own? How might working through those moments be helpful to your child? In what situations might it be more helpful for you to intervene?

3. What age-appropriate responsibilities can you share with your child? Make a list and help your child learn one new task this week.

CHAPTER EIGHT

Know How to Set Your Own Pace

MOMS KEEP A PACE that would rival that of any top business executive. Think about all the hours you put into driving your children all over town for dance, ball, tutoring, music lessons, school, church, outings with friends, doctor visits, dentist appointments, going to see family, and more. That doesn't even include all the school meetings, away games, or vacations. On top of all that, there's the time you working moms put in at your jobs too. To say a mom is busy is an understatement. No wonder most moms are so exhausted they fall into bed so tired they can barely remember to turn off the light.

I understand the pull to stay busy and always have something to do. I can be the world's busiest person! I can cram more stuff in an hour than you would think was humanly possible. The problem with staying so busy is twofold. One, we never build in margin for ourselves to rest and recharge. And two, we miss wonderful opportunities to teach our children life principles. It's not that we don't want to teach them; it's that we're so busy, we don't see the opportunities to teach them.

As I look back on my children's lives, I realize that they opened up to talk to me at the strangest times. Whenever I would ask them, "How was your day at school?" I always got, "It was good." There were never any meaningful conversations in the times I was asking for them. Instead, the meaningful conversations would come late at night when I was tired and ready to go to bed, or early in the morning when my brain wasn't completely awake yet. Sometimes they even wanted to open up to me while I was watching a movie—just when it was getting to the good part! These were the moments they decided felt "right" to open up and share with their mom. And if I hadn't slowed down enough to notice, I would've missed those moments altogether.

Moms, I can speak to the subject of busyness because I have lived it. I have done the "crazy," and I have done a little slower pace. And I will tell you this right now: The slower pace is much more peaceful. Of course, because I had four children, my life may have looked busier than most based solely on the sheer number of people I was caring for. So for our family, I really had to make a decision every year about what pace we would be keeping. I learned early on that the mentality of "I can do it all" didn't work for me.

Instead of doing it for myself, I asked God for wisdom. James 1:5 says this:

> If any of you lacks wisdom, you should ask God, who gives generously to all without finding fault, and it will be given to you.

This became my life verse when my children were small. I did not know how to parent. I was ten hours away from my hometown, and Greg was gone a lot. In other words, I had to depend on God for wisdom. And when I look back now, I realize that God gave me *all* of what

I asked for. I believe He'll do the same for you! But the key is, you have to ask. So ask! Trust me, it's better than burning yourself out.

When Greg got out of active duty with the Navy in 1994, the airlines were not hiring, so he went into the Navy Reserves. This was wonderful because it gave him a paycheck (which we needed). He also switched from the F-14 to the F-18 airplane, meaning he had to go to Florida to learn how to fly the F-18. He would leave every week on Sunday afternoons and not return home again until Friday evenings.

During this time, we were living in a rented house at the beach in Sandbridge, Virginia. It was winter, so the houses were cheap on the bay side of the ocean. I lived in this rented beach house by myself with three small children. Kelsey was four, Emily was two, and Taylor was four months. Taylor was a *big* baby, and I was carrying him everywhere. In our rented house, I would have to go up two flights of stairs to get to the main living quarters, which wore me down. Sandbridge itself was also about 30 minutes from civilized life, which added to the stress of my life. Because it was winter, there was no one at the beach, making it a very lonely place to live.

I kept up our normal lifestyle because I didn't know any better. Despite all that, I truly thought I could do it all and keep my normal pace. Kelsey was in preschool and dance class. I was a table leader at MOPS (Mothers of Preschoolers) on Tuesday mornings at the church. Emily had a Mommy and Me class. We all went to church and Sunday school on Sunday mornings and church again on Wednesday nights. As you can imagine, I was constantly in the car hauling children everywhere. It seemed that no matter how hard I tried to be on time, I was always running late.

Now during this time, Kelsey got very sick. We learned that she had kidney reflux, a condition that meant when she would go the bathroom some of her urine would go back into her kidneys. This was causing kidney damage and would ultimately give her urinary tract infections. So we had to add lots of doctor visits to our routine. Oh, and Taylor had bronchiolitis the first winter of his life, meaning more doctor visits and many sleepless nights. Are you getting the picture? I was physically, mentally, and emotionally worn out.

After several months of this crazy routine, I prayed. I asked God for wisdom. I needed God to guide me on how I was going to keep going because I could not keep that pace up much longer. I felt God tell me to slow down—to drop everything except for the Sunday church services and Kelsey's preschool. So I did. I dropped ballet, MOPS, Wednesday night services, and the toddler class with Emily. At first all I could think of was, *What will people think? I am a MOPS leader. I work in the nursery on Wednesday nights. Emily loves her class with me, and it's the only thing I do with her one-on-one*. Despite all that, I still dropped it. And let me tell you, it was wonderful! It was the best thing I ever did.

My life settled down. I was no longer screaming at my kids to hurry, hurry, hurry and get in the car. I was no longer so worn out at night I could barely read a book at bedtime. I just settled down and got into my routine of staying home with the kids. I learned how to be content in not *going* all the time. I learned to live a very simple life. Up to this point, I'd always tried to fill all the downtime in our schedules. That's just what I thought a mom was supposed to do! My friends put their girls in ballet at three years old, so I did too. I participated in MOPS because that is what other moms did. I was a leader because I had always been a leader. I was young, so in all of it, I just did what was expected of me (or what I thought was expected of me!).

Maybe you're the same way. In our world today, you can get so busy that you stay busy just being busy. Suddenly you're just driving your children everywhere and never getting to the quality time of parenting. What kind of mother or leader was I really being when I screamed at my kids in the car and then showed up to church with a fake smile like it never happened? I was involved in so many things, but I was not doing anything well. When I made the decision to follow God's wisdom and drop a lot of things from our schedule, I began to focus on what was important: my family and myself. And that's so valuable! Because having a great family doesn't just happen; it takes work and determination. You must be focused on the direction your family is going, or it will end up going in a direction you never intended.

This decision really came in handy when the children got into elementary school and I felt that pressure to join everything again. One day Greg and I went to Abby's elementary school to have lunch with her. Greg saw a friend of ours who was volunteering at the school. He said to me, "Do you feel guilty because you never volunteer at the school?" I said, "No, I don't." I shared with him what I had learned a long time ago: I can only do a few things well, and to do those things well, I have to stay focused. My focus was on my husband and my four children. My energy was going toward raising them in a way that would glorify God and, hope-

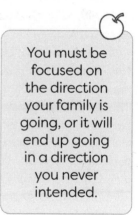

You must be focused on the direction your family is going, or it will end up going in a direction you never intended.

fully, instill in them how much God loved them and wanted a relationship with them. If I accomplished that, I'd feel like I'd done a good job. Getting there was my only focus as a mom.

Moms, I know you may feel like you can't choose this pace and focus for your family, but you can. I know, because I did! My life was different from most people's because of Greg's schedule. Greg was gone 14 to 16 days out of the month, every month. When our children were still in the house, that meant that someone (namely, me) needed to be around to hold down the fort. Because of that one variable, I never worked more than part-time; it didn't work for our family. Sure, there were times I would have liked to have worked more, but when I tried it, the pace got to be too much. It pushed me back toward that crazy cycle that I had desperately left behind.

I know this is tricky, too, because most of us stay busy with "good" things. We aren't filling our days with things that don't matter or that waste our time. But ultimately, we still end up losing. Because even if we're doing a million good things, we end up not being good at anything. None of us wants that, do we? So maybe it's time for us to reevaluate our schedules.

How do we do it? How do we find the balance? How do we stay busy enough without being too busy? I can tell you what I've done, but you can examine the pace of your own family and decide what is best for you. What works for you may not work for me, and that's okay! Get comfortable with *your* pace of life. You are the one setting the pace of your family. Celebrate those who can run at 100 miles an hour, but don't for one second feel like you are less-than because you are not running at that pace. You do you, moms!

It takes a lot of determination and self-examination to stay focused on your family. I've had to give up several good activities because I had too much on my plate. I've also had to give up jobs outside the home because they were taking too much of my time. These were hard decisions (ones I know not everyone can make). Not only were they hard decisions, but our society discourages choices like mine. I had to convince myself that I was not a failure because I couldn't do it all. I would look around and think to myself, *She can do it. Why can't I?* But you cannot worry about what other people are accomplishing with their lives.

Do not believe the voice that tells you that if you are not excelling in a career, or if your children aren't making the honor roll, or if your house will never win a decorating award from *Southern Living*, then you are failing. That's a lie. Satan wants you to doubt your worth. Women think everyone else has it all together, and they are the only ones flying by the seat of their pants. Let me fill you in on a little secret: No one has it all together! We are *all* flying by the seat of our pants, and only with God's grace and wisdom will we make a safe landing! So, give yourself a break. Don't buy into the lie that you have to have it all together. If you did, you wouldn't need a Savior and Lord!

Of course, knowing you need to slow your pace is one thing. Actually doing it is another. So let's talk about three things you can do to slow your pace.

1. Examination

Each year, determine if your family is going in the direction you want to be going. Be honest with yourself. Have your husband do this exercise with you too. Keep every aspect of your family in mind. Does your husband travel? Are your children young? Are they a little older? How many sports are your children involved in during the year? All these things should affect your decisions. The key to slowing down your pace is to realize you actually are in control. You get to say yes or no to the things in your schedule, but you can't do that without first examining what's in your schedule.

As I've said, Greg traveled a lot. He averaged 15 days out of every month his entire career, on the road, so I needed to keep that in mind when examining our schedule. I also had to consider the busier times of the year. For me, the spring was always a busy time. Taylor played golf, starting in middle school, and that activity alone kept us very busy. I tried not to schedule a lot of extra activities during that time of year because of it. When Taylor was transitioning from middle school to high school, he needed extra time at the golf course to be competitive at the high school level. So I made a conscious decision not to put Abby into tennis that year because I simply could not be in two places at one time. At that stage of their lives, I thought it was more important for Taylor to have the activity than Abby. It was a decision I made based on examining my family's schedule and our specific needs.

Of course sacrifices will have to be made when making these decisions. But remember, those sacrifices are worth it. When you see a family you admire because of their family dynamics, chances are it did not just happen that way. That family made some tough choices and sacrifices, and you will have to do the same with your family. You can start figuring out what those are by examining your time and schedule.

2. Action

Putting your plan into action isn't always easy. You might disappoint some people, either your children or friends, when you tell them you aren't going to do a certain sport, or club, or activity. That's okay! You don't have to please everyone. Just keep in mind that you are doing what is best for your family. When I dropped out of MOPS, many of the moms in my group were very disappointed that I was quitting, but I didn't let that stop me. I told them that at that point in my life, I had to slow down. I had too many things on my plate, and it was taking a negative toll on my family. I hated to disappoint any of those women, but at the end of the day I had to do what was best for me and my family. Put your

> If you don't keep your family at the top of your priority list, I assure you, no one else will.

plan into action based on what's best for your family and no one else. Because if you don't keep your family at the top of your priority list, I assure you, no one else will.

When I chose not to put Abby in tennis lessons so Taylor could focus on his golf game, Abby was not happy. Even though I reassured Abby that her day would come, she was like any child. She didn't see the whole picture. She only saw her piece of the pie. Did that make putting our plan into action difficult? Yes! Train yourself to look past emotions and disappointment. Just remember that you are doing what is best for the family.

Listen: You may mess up in some of your decisions, and that's okay too. Keep going. This is your first time parenting those kids, and you are learning as you go. The main thing to keep in mind is that you are making decisions to the best of your ability, and that is a good thing. Learn from your mistakes and missteps and pivot the way you put your plan to action next time.

3. Contentment

This step might be the hardest of all. Contentment means being happy with whatever season of life you are in. Sometimes that's going to be really easy! And other times it just isn't. Remember that contentment is a learned behavior; it doesn't come natural to any of us. Paul says it best here:

> I am not saying this because I am in need, for I have learned to be content whatever the circumstances. I know what it is to be in need, and I know what it is to have plenty. I have learned the secret of being content in any and every situation, whether well fed or hungry, whether living in plenty or in want (Philippians 4:11-12).

Once again, life is made up of seasons. Be flexible and learn to adjust during the different seasons of life. When your kids are toddlers, you will be home a lot because it's just easier. When they are young, you will probably either get a sitter to go out or opt not to go at all. When our children became teenagers, we had to stay at the house all the time to be home for them. We could not go out for a date night because we needed to be home when boys would come to pick up the girls for a date. We needed to be home when they got home too. This new lifestyle really cramped our weekends. So Greg and I started to have our dates on Friday afternoons. In other words, we made adjustments to make it work for our family and still be content.

Those seasons won't last forever, so find contentment in them while you're there. Make adjustments to fit your season of life rather than fight against it. For me, it was so easy to always be looking for the next season and wishing we were there instead where we were. I'm so glad God gave me the wisdom to look for contentment where I was. Otherwise I would've missed out. Stay in the moment of where you are, and don't dream your life away. I promise, children do grow up! They do get older and out from underneath your feet. Each season brings new challenges. Rise to the challenge and make it work for your family at your pace.

REFLECTION QUESTIONS

1. As you pray over your schedule, are there any tasks or responsibilities you feel God calling you to release?

2. How does your current busyness affect your contentment, whether positively or negatively? Would it change if you had less on your schedule?

3. Do your current daily priorities reflect what you believe God wants your priorities to be? If not, what changes should you consider making?

CHAPTER NINE

Know How to Stop Striving for Perfection

WHY DO SO MANY of us strive for perfection? What prize do we believe we'll win if we attain perfection? What does *perfect* really mean, anyway?

Merriam-Webster's dictionary defines *perfect* as "being entirely without fault or defect."[1] Is that what we want as women? As moms? As wives? To be people entirely without faults? Thankfully, we don't have the option. Can we achieve perfection? The answer is obviously no. But if we could achieve perfection, I think it would ultimately make us very lonely.

Let's pretend, by some miracle of miracles, that you one day attain perfection. At some point, someone will come along and mess up your perfect house, your child's perfect outfit, or whatever it was that you accomplished to perfection. And when that person messes up your perfection, what will you do? You'll probably get angry, right? You'll say things you regret, and that person will go away feeling rejected. Then you will be left alone.

I truly believe Satan uses this thinking that perfection might be possible to keep us isolated. As long as we have the false belief that

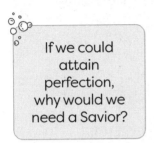

If we could attain perfection, why would we need a Savior?

we must be perfect, act perfectly, and live perfectly in order to be loved, we will never live the Christian life the way we should. Gently remind yourselves that all our needs are met in Christ Jesus (Philippians 4:19). In other words, if we could attain perfection, why would we need a Savior?

This concept really burdens my heart. The goal of perfection can never be achieved, and the pursuit of it always leaves women feeling inadequate. I get angry with our society, which encourages us to strive for perfection. Social media alone paints this beautiful, perfect picture of families and moms. But here is the deal: Those pictures people are posting, are just that—pictures. How quickly we forget those are just pictures! We begin to believe that those pictures are the way those people live all the time and not just a highlight. People post the "best" of everything. No one ever posts a picture on social media of their child having a meltdown in the grocery store, or their living room that looks like a toy explosion happened, or their high school student's failed grade. Social media is one big advertising tool. How many times have I gotten caught up in seeing someone decorate their table with this beautiful arrangement and I go to the store and get the exact decorations, only to find out that I can't make it look anything like what I saw on social media? What happens to my self-confidence after that? You guessed it: It's in the tank.

Now, take a young mom with little children who is scrolling one afternoon and sees beautiful pictures of a friend's family, with the children looking beyond perfect in their matching outfits, beautiful smiles on their faces and just looking angelic. That sweet mom is going to beat herself up and convince herself that she doesn't have what it takes—that she must not be a good mom. That mom will more than likely waste at least an hour of her time scrolling and feeling like she's not enough. The enemy has won. Do you see the correlation? Even if someone "looks" perfect, I guarantee you, they are not.

So I am giving you permission to not be perfect. Your children do not have to be perfect, your home does not have to be perfect, your marriage doesn't have to be perfect, and you, don't have to be perfect. For some of you, this brings a sigh of relief. For others—my perfectionists out there—this will be more difficult to take in. Because you not only look for perfection in yourself; you look for perfection in your children as well. But just like you will never be a perfect parent, they will never be perfect children. They will never be able to measure up to your standard. They will never be able to sustain a perfect life.

When I was a little girl, I loved my grandma on my father's side of the family. We called her Grandmother (real original, I know). Grandmother was a widow, and my dad was an only child. So we were all she had to love, and love us she did. She was always proud of us, no matter how small or great our accomplishments. Grandmother was the picture of unconditional love. Grandmother never expected us to be perfect; she accepted us just the way we were. In return, we all loved her dearly. I pray that I have those characteristics as a mom to my own children. I pray my children will know that I love them in their imperfection.

When I was a young mom, I admit that I wanted the picture-perfect family. I wanted people to look at us and think, *Oh my heavens, that is the cutest, sweetest family in the world!* Now mind you, this was way before social media, so my little corner of the world truly was only as big as my church and neighborhood friends. For a long time I strived for that standard of perfection. But I think God broke me of the desire to be perfect when I had my son, Taylor. Before Taylor was born, I had two girls. They loved dressing up and being girly, so I could dress them any way I wanted. Then I had Taylor, a son who was all boy. He was so cute! With his white-blonde hair and big, brown eyes, he could melt your heart with one glance. But Taylor definitely liked to dress a certain way—one that usually didn't line up with my idea of perfection at all!

Taylor had a pair of cowboy boots, and he wanted to wear them all the time. He even liked wearing them in the summer heat! He would wear those cowboy boots to church with his shorts and a T-shirt, and there wasn't anything I could do to stop him. And it didn't stop with the boots! When he started elementary school, some mornings Taylor would leave the house without combing his hair. I was horrified! But when I finally gave up trying to make him look perfect and accepted him for who he was (boots and all), our relationship improved tremendously.

Like so many young moms, I struggled to relax. In fact, along the way, I had to learn to allow myself to relax. As I mentioned before, my rule was to stop working around the house after 8:00 p.m. If there was laundry to do, it would have to wait until the next day. If dishes needed to be washed, they would have to wait. From 8:00 p.m. until the next morning, I would relax, enjoy some time with Greg, and just chill. And you know what I discovered? Relaxing is a lot more fun than being an uptight perfectionist. I mean, who wants to be a nag? I didn't want to be a mom who was constantly nagging my kids and fussing at my husband. After a while, they stop hearing it anyway. I would rather be heard and make a difference than have my kids rolling their eyes, thinking, *Here she goes again!*

If you are one of the many moms out there who struggles with a desire to be perfect, let me give you a tip: Put your efforts in perfection toward perfecting your walk with God. Put your energies and emotions into being the best child of God you can be. Start every day by saying, "God, let me be poured-out wine and broken bread for You. I want Your will to be done in my life more than my own will. I pray that there would be less of me and more of You." If you commit to this prayer, it will help you die to yourself and your image of perfection every day. And over time, your marriage, your children, and your home will be better because of it.

Put your efforts in perfection toward perfecting your walk with God.

In most areas in my life, I'm not wired toward perfection. That is not good or bad; it is just the way I am wired. I am the third out of four children, and my sister, Riki, is seven years younger than me. Translation: I was treated like the baby of the family for seven years. The baby of any family typically adopts a carefree, easygoing, and very positive outlook. Youngest children don't have that many burdens on them because they realize there are other people worrying about stuff for them. These are the characteristics I took on as a child, and I carried them into most parts of my adult life. But now I have a child who struggles with perfectionism and a husband who is a perfectionist too. So what I haven't experienced myself, I've observed in them over the years.

And what have I learned? That there are dangers in pursuing perfection. Yes, we should all strive to do our best in life. Colossians 3:17 says,

> Whatever you do in word or deed, do everything in the name of the Lord Jesus, giving thanks through Him to God the Father (NASB).

This verse makes it clear that God wants us to do our best—to work hard at achieving excellence. There is a fine line, though, between doing our best and trying to be perfect. It is very easy to cross over to the other side, and if some of us have these tendencies, we should be aware of the danger that lies ahead.

I want to share what I believe are three destructive outcomes of the pursuit of perfection.

1. Disappointment

The first destructive result of perfectionism is disappointment. If perfectionism is our goal, we will always go away feeling like failures. We're always going to think we just don't measure up. What a horrible way to live! And worst of all? When we live disappointed—when we feel like failures—we invite Satan to get a victory in our lives.

Greg has accomplished so much in his life. He graduated from Georgia Tech as a mechanical engineer and went on to become a fighter pilot in the US Navy. He was also a Top Gun graduate and was top in his squadron. He then got a job with FedEx and has been doing that successfully since 1994. But with all that success, he still struggles to see he hasn't failed. Somehow it is still not enough for him. No matter how much Greg accomplishes, he thinks he could have accomplished more. Do you see how destructive that way of thinking can be? It is a lie that Satan places in our minds, and it will destroy us if we allow it to rule our lives.

God does not accept us because of what we accomplish or "do" for Him; He cares about who we are on the inside. When my daughter Kelsey lived with us, she had a sign hanging in her room that said, "I love you more because of who you are than what you do." Kelsey tends to be a perfectionist, and this sign was a daily reminder to her that God cares more about her heart than her accomplishments. It is easy to lose sight of this truth, isn't it? We get so focused on whether things are perfect that we forget about what is important to God: our hearts. Only His Son is perfect, and through Jesus, not through our own accomplishments, we will find our peace and joy.

2. Destruction of Relationships

The second destructive result of perfectionism is that it can ruin our relationships. If we lean toward perfectionism, we will probably transfer this to our children, whether we mean to or not. After a while, they will either stop trying because they'll realize they can never achieve our standards or they will become perfectionists, just like us. I had a friend who vacuumed her house twice a day, every day. There is nothing wrong with vacuuming your house twice a day, of course! But this friend also had two young children. So this habit taught her children that it was very important not to mess up the carpet. And as a result, they couldn't relax in their own home. This isn't how we want our kids to feel, is it? Do we want to live in shrines to perfection? Or do we want warm, loving homes that are always open and welcoming?

Perfectionism puts expectations on our kids that are too great a burden for them.

Perfectionism puts expectations on our kids that are too great a burden for them. Please do not misunderstand me. I believe that we should teach our kids to do their best and to strive for excellence in all that they do. But we must also understand that there is a balance. And if we don't find the balance, it will be destructive to our relationships with our children.

Greg and I always wanted our kids to make As in school. Kelsey struggled in math; some years she would make an A, and some years she would make a B. Even though we wanted her to make an A, we knew that sometimes a B was the best she could do. Emily, on the other hand, could make As in math but struggled in English. Our goal was for all our kids to do their best. Sometimes that meant an A, and sometimes it meant a B. Rather than force perfection on our kids, we chose to encourage them simply to do their best.

We don't ever want our kids to feel like they can't do enough to make us happy. If they do, they will give up completely. This brings me to my lifelong saying: "Everything in moderation!" And yes, that even includes our expectations for our kids. I believe it is important as parents that we realize and accept that our children are growing and learning. Emphasize that they should always do their best, not be perfect.

3. Self-Sufficiency

The third destructive pattern is self-sufficiency, which leads to a lack of reliance on God. Perfectionism instills the belief that getting something accomplished the right way is up to the individual. So if that individual does not do the job perfectly, they have failed. One lesson I tried to teach my kids is that they needed to do each job given to them the best they could, then ask God to do the rest. I wanted them to realize their dependence on God and not to ever believe they were in control. I wanted them to understand God's sovereignty. It would be such a gift if our kids could realize this principle: *God is in control, and, therefore, I don't have to be in control.* Wouldn't we love for them to learn at an early age to rest in the Lord? How powerful that would be!

Whether you are a perfectionist or not, you probably still struggle with balancing housework, husband, children, cooking, cleaning, and everything else. The list goes on and on; it is *never* finished. Just when we think we've finished that last load of laundry, one of our kids will walk through the door and dump out a pile of clothes that have been sitting in his gym locker at school. That picture is anything but perfect, right?

Once again, balance is key. It's okay if you don't finish your to-do list in one day. And it's okay if you don't finish it perfectly! Remember, focus on doing your best in the season you're in. One day the craziness will come to an end. Don't give up or get discouraged. You are doing a *great* job!

REFLECTION QUESTIONS

1. What impossible standards have you set for yourself? What about for your children? Or for your husband? What drives you to want to hold on to goals you can't realistically achieve?

2. How have you experienced the fallout of perfectionism? When has perfectionism stopped you from pursuing better goals, relationships, or habits?

3. What areas of control are you holding onto that you can (and should) release to God? How can regular prayer over this struggle help you do this?

CHAPTER TEN

Know How to Rest in Your Identity in Christ

MERRIAM-WEBSTER'S DICTIONARY defines *self-worth* as "a sense of one's own value as a human being."[1] It is important that you as a woman know your value. You bring a lot to the table of being a parent. You have many talents and giftings to offer to your child and family, and most important, you have a loving nurturing side that your child desperately needs. It is easy in motherhood to stop valuing yourself because you can feel like you are never measuring up to the expectations you put on yourself, or what you feel society is putting on you. Don't allow those expectations to dictate how you feel about yourself. We've talked about how many moms feel less-than when they are scrolling through social media. They see beautiful, talented women, doing so much with their lives or for their children, and they start to compare themselves to those images on social media.

Comparing ourselves to anyone is never good. It will only take us to a bad place mentally. The problem with comparing is that you either determine that you are better than someone else or worse than someone else. Either way, you're wrong.

Again, I guarantee that no mom has it completely together, no matter how much it looks like she does. We are all in need of a Savior. God has given us different gifts, meaning no one is the complete package. God did not design us, the body of believers, to function this way. He has specifically gifted each one of us with different gifts so we might work together as one unit.

> Our bodies are made up of many parts. None of these parts have the same use. There are many people who belong to Christ. And yet, we are one body which is Christ's. We are all different but we depend on each other. We all have different gifts that God has given to us by His loving-favor. We are to use them. If someone has the gift of preaching the Good News, he should preach. He should use the faith God has given him. If someone has the gift of helping others, then he should help. If someone has the gift of teaching, he should teach. If someone has the gift of speaking words of comfort and help, he should speak. If someone has the gift of sharing what he has, he should give from a willing heart. If someone has the gift of leading other people, he should lead them. If someone has the gift of showing kindness to others, he should be happy as he does it (Romans 12:4-8 NLV).

Listen, I am a better woman because God has given me friends who are very talented in areas where I am not. I have become a more well-rounded person just by having them in my life. If I ever start to become jealous, I realize that is Satan messing with me. So I tell him to leave because he is not welcome in my life. Then, to shift my focus, I thank God for blessing me with the gifts He has given me.

I realize in motherhood you might need a little more direction on how you can see your worth. Let's be real: We all need help here! Hardly any of us see our worth the way God intended us to see it. So I'd love to map out exactly how we can get there. Please keep in mind, this is a process. It will not happen overnight, but over a lifetime. The good news is, God sees you today and He loves you! And because of that He wants to help you see yourself the way He does. He wants you to find your worth in Him.

So, how can we value ourselves? Here are a few things to try.

1. Celebrate Who You Are

God created you just the way you are. Psalm 139:13 says,

> You created my inmost being; you knit me together in my mother's womb.

Let's just think about this verse for a minute. The God of the universe created you! He knit you together in your mother's womb. He gave you exactly what He wanted you to have. Your eyes, your hair, your body type, your brain, your personality—He created it all. That means you are special!

And in Psalm 139:14, we find this truth:

> I praise you because I am fearfully and wonderfully made;
> your works are wonderful, I know that full well.

Don't gloss over these verses. Sit and meditate on them. Everything about you was made on purpose. You may think, *Why is that so important?* Well, it's important because what you believe about yourself reflects in everything you do. It affects how you see the world, how you parent your children, how you love others, and how you love yourself. I know we all have things about ourselves that we would like to change, but God made us the way we are. When we see that as a gift, we find new freedom to celebrate who we are.

God created you just the way you are, and He does not make mistakes. If every mom would embrace that truth, it would have a huge impact on the next generation. Imagine what our society would look like if we were all confident in the way God made us. If I can communicate this truth to my children and see them really get it, I will feel truly successful as a mom! But I cannot pass these thoughts on to my children unless I believe them myself. I have to change my way of thinking; then I will have influence in their lives.

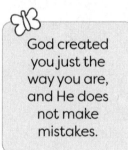

God created you just the way you are, and He does not make mistakes.

Ladies, think of it! Being in a room full of other moms and being confident in who you are. Not sizing up the other women. Knowing those women might have more talent in certain areas than you and being okay with that. Instead of becoming resentful or jealous, actually celebrating with those women. How wonderful would that be? What a gift to ourselves, to other women, and to our children if we can adopt this mindset!

I used to tell my children this principle all the time. They would cry about wanting to be prettier, or wishing they didn't have to wear glasses, or wanting to have some sort of talent or ability, and I would tell them,

"God created you just the way you are, and He doesn't make mistakes. Be thankful for the way you are." I've mentioned that my little Abby wore glasses from the time she was 15 months old. Her prescription was very strong, so her glasses were thick. When she was in elementary school, people would comment on her glasses and tell her that her eyes looked like frog eyes. Of course she was insecure about her eyes. But when we'd talk about it, I would share these verses with her, letting her know that God allowed her eyes to be the way they are for a reason. Maybe that reason was so she would be compassionate toward others. Maybe it was so she'd never make fun of someone else because she knew what it felt like to be made fun of herself. I didn't know the exact reason, but I knew she was fearfully and wonderfully made. I knew she was special just the way she was, and I wanted her to know that too.

It's the same with you. God made you just the way He wanted you to be, and that is something to celebrate. Celebrate *you*! Celebrate your whole self, even the stuff you want to change. Celebrate your body, your personality, your looks. Celebrate your life because it is worth celebrating. Give thanks to God every day for your life, your family, and the opportunities He's given you on this earth.

2. Run Your Own Race

I tell moms all the time that we each have a race set out for us. Hebrews 12:1 says it this way:

> Since we are surrounded by such a great cloud of witnesses,
> let us throw off everything that hinders and the sin that so
> easily entangles. And let us run with perseverance the race
> marked out for us.

My race will look different from your race, and your race will be different from mine. That is okay! What boring lives we would have if we all ran the same race! So stay in your lane and work hard not to be distracted by the other racehorses around you.

Did you know that racehorses wear blinders to stay focused? It helps them stay in their lanes. It gives them a shot at running a better race. We can learn to do the same. To put our blinders on and stay in our own lanes. Don't look at people to your left or right, but stay focused on the lane God has given you. Run *your* race!

It took me years to finally be content with my lane. I would look around and want another person's life, or house, or job, or possessions, or even her relationships. I'm not proud of that, but I want to be honest about it. God showed me over the years to stop looking at others—to stop comparing. Why? Because it wasn't doing me any good. Remember, Paul tells us that contentment is a learned behavior (Philippians 4:11). We have to work at it every day. And we won't get very far if we're looking at everyone else all the time.

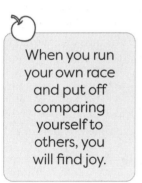

When you run your own race and put off comparing yourself to others, you will find joy.

Running your own race brings freedom and joy. Freedom to live the life you are supposed to live without jealousy or envy. Freedom to run with no burdens attached. When you run your own race and put off comparing yourself to others, you will find joy. Joy just doesn't happen, but when you are focusing on your own life and not looking at the lives of others,

you'll find it, step by step. Of course that takes discipline. Walking with the Lord will help your heart here. Walking daily with God, asking for His help and wisdom, praying that the fruits of the Spirit will begin to flow out of you—these are great places to start!

I speak from experience. A lot of people in my life are way smarter than me, more talented than me, and have so much more than me. But I have learned to encourage them in their race while staying happy and content in my lane.

3. Know Your Strengths and Weaknesses

When you know your strengths and weaknesses, you will be happier and more productive and get along with others more easily. If a person doesn't know their strengths and weaknesses, they will more than likely live out of their weaknesses all the time. They'll just stay frustrated at themselves because they are trying to be something they are not. They don't know what they're good at to even begin with, so they aren't sure the best place to operate from.

I had a friend in Virginia who was very talented with arts and crafts. She could make a shoe box into a work of art with some glue and glitter. I told her she really had a gift, and she replied that I was gifted in that area too. I told her I was not, but that was okay. I knew my strengths (and I definitely knew my weaknesses!). And more than that, I was okay with both.

If you have a friend who is very gifted in a certain area, don't beat yourself up because you're not. Instead, celebrate that with her. Know your gifts, and don't feel like you have to be all things to all people. I might not have the gift of organization, but I do have the gifts of hospitality and encouragement. And because I know my gifts, I can take them and partner with people who have what I don't. Together, we can do some great things for God.

I learned to apply this principle in my marriage too. As I said before, Greg is very organized. He is methodical, and life for him has a purpose. I, on the other hand, can be very creative and spontaneous. During the first years of our marriage, we would struggle with each other. He was always trying to get me to be more like him, and I was determined that he would not take away my creative, fun side. Neither one of us would give in to the other, which created tension. Then we went to a marriage retreat with our church. The speaker had struggled in his marriage with the very same issues for years. He told us that they learned to take their opposite traits and combine them to make one strong force as a team. We decided to adopt this new way of thinking, and it changed our marriage completely. From then on, instead of Greg trying to get me to be more like him, he celebrated the way I was made. And I did the same for him. I no longer felt like I was competing with him. Instead, I saw us as a team, drawing help from each other in places we were lacking.

We all can and should work together as the body of Christ. God never intended for us to work independently. It's His design that we work together in one Spirit. That's why it's also important that we know when to ask for help. Because we all need help from time to time. You don't have to be a superhero, so ask for help when you need it. Know your limits. Ask for help when you're operating out of your weaknesses. Trust me, you'll be thankful you did!

And finally, embrace who *you* are as a woman. If you are not the type of mom who likes to get on the floor and play with your children, own it. I'll own it; that was not the way I'm wired. Greg could play for hours with the children and now the grandchildren, but that is not me. I can play "tea party" for about five to ten minutes, and then I'm done. Instead of apologizing for it, I'm owning it! And you should do the same.

Embrace who you are. Be true to yourself. Find confidence and worth in the unique person—the unique parent—God made you to be. Stay in that sweet spot, and you'll be a better mom.

REFLECTION QUESTIONS

1. What makes you feel less-than? When do you most struggle with comparison? What strategies can you use to fight against this temptation?

2. Read Psalm 139:13-14. How does this passage encourage you to celebrate who you are and the identity God has given you?

3. What are your areas of strengths and weaknesses? How do your friends' strengths complement yours? What's one way you can encourage them by celebrating the gifts God has given them?

If You Know Nothing Else, Know God

I HOPE YOU HAVE BEEN encouraged and challenged in reading this book. It has been a joy to share my journey with you here.

Why do I write to moms? Because I want you to know you are not alone. And with that, I want to give you hope for the future. Hopefully in reading these real-life stories from a fellow mom, you'll realize that you can do this journey of motherhood. Even if life throws you a few curveballs along the way, God will guide you through it.

You might be wondering how things are going for our family now. After her seventh surgery, Kelsey started to heal and recover, and in February 2019, she and her family moved to Corpus Christi, Texas. When Kelsey and her children moved in with us in March of 2018, I thought my role as the mom and grandmother was to help her get through Kevin's deployment until she delivered the baby. But God knew it would become so much more than that.

I was balancing three young children (one being a newborn!), the ministry of Birds on a Wire, helping my mom and sisters take my dad to the doctor for treatments, and running my own house. I kept thinking to myself, *If I can just get to the next month, things will get better.* But things didn't get better in the way I'd hoped. Yes, Kelsey's health got better, but my father's health declined. By Thanksgiving, my dad's cancer was stage 4, and he passed away December 21, 2018.

When I look back on that year, I know it was one of the hardest times in my life. But I also see it as a season when God carried me through. We tell ourselves all the time that God will not put more on us than we can bear, but that's just not true. In fact, that's not found in Scripture at all. There were many times I didn't feel I could handle anything else, but in those times, I found God's strength all the more. He provided support in so many areas—through people, prayers, food provided, and a wonderful family to lean on during the hard days. God got me through. Life is not always pleasant or fun. If you live long enough, you will go through dark days, but you'll also realize that those days will not last forever. And more than anything, God is with you, even in the darkest days.

I now am back to the empty-nester stage of life and have adjusted to a quieter lifestyle. Greg and I are enjoying these days together, planning and dreaming of the next trip we will be going on together. All four of my children are married now, and I love the friendships that I have with my adult children. I also love being a grandmother to Evie (10), Chapman (8), Talon (5), Harper (5), Grayson (3) and little baby girl Stubbs arriving in 2024. I truly love watching my children be parents, and I think it helps keep me relevant in the mom world because I see it firsthand with my grandchildren. Emily is now my cohost on the podcast *Wire Talk* and that has been a fun journey. God continues to be faithful and blesses Birds on a Wire as we equip and encourage moms all over the world.

Be encouraged, moms! Your family and friends may not see all that you do, but your heavenly Father does. He loves and cares for you deeply. Lean into Him in your mothering journey, and He will direct your path!

I hope you enjoyed this book and the bottom lines of motherhood shared within. If you were to walk away with just one thought—one truth to hold on to in your journey of motherhood—it would be this: *Know God.*

Knowing God will anchor you in every phase of the journey. So lean into Him, trust Him, and continue to walk with Him as you go. Enjoy the journey, moms. It is a wild ride to be sure!

Love,

Karen

Acknowledgments

WE ALL HAVE PEOPLE in our lives who need to be acknowledged for helping us get to where we are, and I am no different. I want to thank my dear husband, Greg. I could not have asked for a better husband and cheerleader. Thank you for always being willing to share all our stories—the good and the bad—to help relate to moms and encourage them. The writing process is never an easy one, and when I wanted to give up, you would push me to keep going. You have believed in me since day one, and I am lucky to have you in my corner. Thank you!

I cannot say thank you enough to my four children, who love and support all I do for moms. You have given me permission to share your stories of growing up, which sometimes don't paint a pretty picture. Thank you for allowing me to share, to help moms not feel alone in their journey of motherhood.

Thank you to the entire team at Harvest House. Thank you for believing in me and this book. Your help and encouragement along the way have been amazing!

Last, I want to thank God for meeting me where I was as a young mom, loving me, and guiding me through the journey. You gave me wisdom when I asked, and for that I am very grateful. I love the verse in Isaiah 40:11: "He gently leads those that have young." This verse is true for me and all moms. Thank You!

Notes

Chapter Three: Know How to Keep Your Sanity

1. The Britannica Dictionary, s.v. "sacrifice (n.)," accessed October 20, 2023, https://www.britannica.com/dictionary/sacrifice.

Chapter Four: Know How to Stay Connected with Your Spouse

1. *Merriam-Webster*, s.v. "martyr (n.)," accessed October 20, 2023, https://www.merriam-webster.com/dictionary/martyr.

2. Karen Stubbs, interview with Dr. Mike Sytsma, *Wire Talk*, podcast audio, October 2, 2018, https://birdsonawiremoms.com/podcast/episode131.

Chapter Six: Know How to Be a Student of Your Child

1. **General Personality Episodes:**

How Do I Parent Different Personality Types?
birdsonawiremoms.com/podcast/episode15
What Are the Different Personality Types?
birdsonawiremoms.com/podcast/episode60
Red, Yellow, Green or Blue? How to Parent the Kids God Gave You
birdsonawiremoms.com/podcast/episode103
Understanding Your Child's Temperament (Their "Color")
birdsonawiremoms.com/podcast/episode283
The What, the How, and the Why of the Personality Colors
birdsonawiremoms.com/podcast/episode329

Episodes Dealing with One Specific Personality Color - KIDS

How Do I Parent My "Red" Strong-Willed Child?
birdsonawiremoms.com/podcast/episode121
Gaining Understanding of Our "Greens"
birdsonawiremoms.com/podcast/episode132

Help! My "Blue" Kid Is Making Me Melancholy
birdsonawiremoms.com/podcast/episode136
Little Miss Sunshine—Parenting Your Yellow Child
birdsonawiremoms.com/podcast/episode145

Episodes Dealing with One Specific Personality - MOMS

Thriving As a Calm & Peaceful Green Mom
birdsonawiremoms.com/podcast/episode152
Letting Go of Your Need for Control as a Red Mom
birdsonawiremoms.com/podcast/episode157
Help for the Perfection-Seeking Blue Mom
birdsonawiremoms.com/podcast/episode160
Playing to Your Strengths as a Yellow Mom
birdsonawiremoms.com/podcast/episode164

Episodes Dealing with One Specific Personality - DAD

An Interview with Two "Peaceful" Green Dads
birdsonawiremoms.com/podcast/episode368
An Interview with Two "Perfect" Blue Dads
birdsonawiremoms.com/podcast/episode369
An Interview with Two "Powerful" Red Dads
birdsonawiremoms.com/podcast/episode370
An Interview with Two "Playful" Yellow Dads
birdsonawiremoms.com/podcast/episode371

2. The first person I found who was teaching the colors was Teresa Gilbert, based on Personality Patch training found at www.PathwaysToExcellence.net.

Chapter Nine: Know to Stop Striving for Perfection

1. *Merriam-Webster*, s. v. "perfect," accessed October 20, 2023, https://www.merriam-webster .com/dictionary/perfect.

Chapter Ten: Know How to Rest in Your Identity in Christ

1. *Merriam-Webster*, s.v., "self-worth," accessed October 20, 2023, https://www.merriam -webster.com/dictionary/self-worth.